**SpringerBriefs in Law**

More information about this series at http://www.springer.com/series/10164

Alexander Wellerdt

# Organisation of Banking Regulation

Springer

Alexander Wellerdt
Hamburg
Germany

ISSN 2192-855X ISSN 2192-8568 (electronic)
SpringerBriefs in Law
ISBN 978-3-319-17637-6 ISBN 978-3-319-17638-3 (eBook)
DOI 10.1007/978-3-319-17638-3

Library of Congress Control Number: 2015936292

Springer Cham Heidelberg New York Dordrecht London


Printed on acid-free paper

Springer International Publishing AG Switzerland is part of Springer Science+Business Media
(www.springer.com)

# Preface

The following study on the organisation of banking regulation has arisen during a stay at the Deutsche Bundesbank from August to October 2014. Further developments of the legal framework and monetary policies could be taken into consideration until February 2015.

I would like at this point put on record my gratefulness for the support provided by colleagues and friends and their willingness to engage in vivid dialogues.

First, I offer my sincerest gratitude to Dr. Daniel Rau and Dr. Christian Heidfeld of the Deutsche Bundesbank, who took an active part in discussing—critically and passionately—legal issues on banking regulation.

I also want to thank Prof. Dr. Thomas Wein and his colleagues Dr. Annika Pape and Mr. Arne Neukirch of the Institut für Volkswirtschaftslehre of the University of Lüneburg for their willingness to communicate and their careful remarks on the complex interaction of the monetary policy.

I would particularly like to thank Lara Bartels and Bianca Griepe, who greatly supported this work linguistically.

I thank Springer Verlag and especially Dr. Brigitte Reschke for the inclusion of this work in the *SpringerBriefs in Law* series as well as the efficient and professional support of the publication.

Moreover, I thank Dr. Klaus Schleicher for his generous sponsorship of this project.

Finally, I thank Christiane and Jörg, Lena and Nepomuk as well as Alexander for your amicable contributions that made work easier and your constant motivation that kept me going.

Lüneburg/Heidelberg, February 2015 Alexander Wellerdt

# Preface

# Contents

# Chapter 1
# Introduction

> ***Does organization matter?*** Scharpf, Does Organization Matter? Task Structure and Interaction in the Ministerial Bureaucracy, Organization and Administrative Sciences (1977), 149.

In the European Composite Administration, the density of material rules increased in many economic sectors. The application and enforcement of these rules ought to be administered by formal organisations. "*Does organisation matter*?" can be clearly answered favourable. In fact, organisations begin to receive the attention they deserve.

Administrative organisation is no end in itself. In fact it is required for each administrative action. In a multi polar, supranational and administrative surrounding the administrative organisation grows in importance in several economic sectors and life areas. Administrative organisation is regarded as being static and boring—the opposite is the case. Administrative organisations are influential. They take in external influences to react flexible to changes in time. Administrative organisations help to fulfil public services at its best.

Thus, this thesis studies the administration and its organisation. The thesis is based on the "reference area"[1] of banking regulation at national, European and international level. Regulation is one of the youngest dogmatic and most creative tasks of administration and increasingly presents administrative action. Regulation leads to a greater need of information to meet diverse consulting and decision-making situations of administration. This particularly applies to areas of asymmetric information between the administration of regulation and regulated economic sectors. Thereby, administration and its previous organisation are challenged to develop. Organisation matters!

---

[1]Coining of the term Schmidt-Aßmann, Das Allgemeine Verwaltungsrecht als Ordnungsidee, 2nd ed. (Springer, 2004); Ch.1.paras.12 et seq. and Ch. 3. paras. 1 et seq.; with the help of a reference area, a real area of administrative organisation is processed specially to detect the developments at national and European level, Terhechte, Einführung: Das Verwaltungsrecht der Europäischen Union als Gegenstand rechtswissenschaftlicher Forschung - Entwicklungslinien, Prinzipien und Perspektiven, in Terhechte (Ed.), Verwaltungsrecht der Europäischen Union, (Nomos, 2010), § 1 para. 62.

 
A. Wellerdt, *Organisation of Banking Regulation*, SpringerBriefs in Law,
DOI 10.1007/978-3-319-17638-3_1

## 1.1 Subject of the Study

Regulation includes any sovereign interference of administration in an economic sector. Regulation is especially important in the financial markets. Only in October 2008 the business behaviour of financial institutions lead to a global collapse of the market. The causes and consequences are diverse and still present.

### *1.1.1 Introduction*

So far, the regulation of the financial markets followed a strategy of self-regulation. States agreed on non-binding standards and thus provided a framework which was put into practice by the financial sector with less government control and without government valuation. As a result, financial institutions set a focus on returns and neglected risks. This particular business behaviour of financial institutions was endeavoured by an expansionary monetary policy of the U.S. Federal Reserve. Cheap money at low interest rates was supposed to boost bank lending to private clients. Through a lack of market discipline, while granting credits against securities (mortgage), a bubble in the housing market emerged. The creditworthiness or liquidity of clients and the value of real estate as collateral were overestimated.[2] Long-dated loans were bundled by banks and then resold (to regional banks, life insurance companies, pension funds and investment banks).[3] So-called Asset-Backed-Securities were structured with graded default risks and varying interest rates were rated positive (AAA-Rating) by rating agencies. Default or liability risks could not be measured reliably,[4] and loan securitisations were laid with less equity than securities in the balance sheets.[5] This business behaviour was particularly favoured by commercial and investment banks. They provided false incentives to run risky financial activities and also paid large bonuses to employees.[6]

Increasing defaults in payment by borrowers led to price reductions of credit securitisation. Rating agencies downgraded the ratings and revealed an inadequate availability of capital and liquidity constraints in the financial institutions. The collapse of single financial institutions led, on the one hand, to a huge loss of

[2]Hellwig, Gutachten zum 68. Deutschen Juristentag, (C.H. Beck, 2010), E12 et seq.; 20 et seq.

[3]Hellwig, Gutachten zum 68. Deutschen Juristentag, (C.H. Beck, 2010), E12 et seq.; 16 et seq.

[4]Hellwig, Gutachten zum 68. Deutschen Juristentag, (C.H. Beck, 2010), E22 et seq.

[5]Hellwig, Gutachten zum 68. Deutschen Juristentag, (C.H. Beck, 2010), E31 et seq.

[6]R. Fischer in Boos/Fischer/Schulte-Mattler (Eds.), KWG, 4th ed. (C.H. Beck, 2012), Einf KWG (German Banking Act) para.103.

confidence in the soundness of the banking system and, on the other hand, to a liquidity crisis.[7] Large or specialised credit institutions were about to become insolvent. However, these institutions were deemed to be too big to fail.[8]

Governmental assistance was required to preserve the functioning of the economy.[9] This idea enjoyed politically a broad consensus but was economically not without controversy. In a market economy, governmental interventions are an exception. If government agencies provide financial assistance to rescue banks, these banks are no longer forced to leave the market, even if they operated poorly. Governmental assistance favours single institutions rather than bringing economic resources to their best use by free market forces. Thus, the competition is distorted and damaged. Supply and demand are no longer allocated efficiently. Market failures occur which were accompanied by insufficient supervision and a lack of regulations to execute bank resolutions and insolvencies. These deficits in regulation and supervision had a systemic effect and lead to government failure.[10] The self-regulation of financial markets failed. Financial institutions are operating across borders at the European internal market. Nevertheless, the supervision of business behaviour takes place at a national level and is subject of widely varying regulations between the Member States.[11] The banking crisis has shown that financial institutions engaged in risky speculation while trusting that the government and therefore the taxpayers will give, if necessary, a helping hand. Incentives like taking a higher risk than economically efficient (moral hazard)[12] have a macroeconomic impact and burden the acceptance of the market economy system. In response to the shortcomings and failures of the financial sector a more consistent and comprehensive state regulation developed. Based on the structural causes of the crisis, the Banking Regulation Law tightened the substantive rules at a supranational level. First, the capital adequacy requirements were increased to underpin high-risk positions, also liquidity principles were specified and their implementation monitored by stress tests.[13] In this way, the risks of a bank solvency are reduced, a new

---

[7]In particular after the collapse of both the IKB in July 2007 in Germany and the investment bank Lehman Brothers Banking Corporation in the United States in September of 2008.

[8]The term too big to fail describes companies whose insolvency would cost the national economy more than its rescue. According to the Financial Stability Board, 28 banks and nine insurance companies are currently considered to be so large that their collapse would threaten the financial system, Bundesanstalt für Finanzdienstleistungsaufsicht, Systemrelevante Finanzunternehmen, BaFin-Journal 10/2013, 30 (31).

[9]In Germany there is to name in particular the "rescue" of the Hypo Real Estate with guarantees from the government in the amount of 100 billion euros and the participation of the Federal Government as a shareholder of the Commerzbank.

[10]Kindler, Finanzkrise und Finanzmarktregulierung, Neue Juristische Wochenschrift (2010), 2465.

[11]Ferber, Die Neuordnung der europäischen Aufsichtsstruktur, Ifo-Schnelldienst 64 (2011), 9 (10).

[12]In particular explored in the securities market: Mankiw and Taylor (Eds.), Economics, 2nd ed. (South Western Cengage Learning, 2011), 823; Bormann and Finsinger (Eds.), Markt und Regulierung, (Vahlen, 1999), 512 et seq.

[13]An overview is provided by Zeitler, Finanzmarktkrise und Bankenaufsicht, in Grieser and Heemann (Eds.), Bankenaufsichtsrecht, (Frankfurt School Verlag, 2010), 5.

confidence between banks can be created and the interbank market is stimulated. Moreover, the formally established independent supervisory structure provides sanctions, and combines the supervision at both macroeconomic and microeconomic level.[14] Especially here, the administrative organisation grows in importance.

### *1.1.2 Framing of the Problem*

The administrative organisation creates the structural requirements for the administration.[15] Particularly, the design of organisational units enables a context control. The control of administrative actions by organisations happens within a standardised framework. These frameworks affect the decision-making processes of administrative units, which affect in return the ability to make certain types of administrative actions or decisions.[16] Administrative organisation is attached to a growing importance not only formally, but also materially. The Administrative Organisation Law creates structures in which regulatory decisions are controlled.

The organisational law of the administration of regulation is not recognised appropriately in jurisprudential discussion. It rather runs out in the mere descriptions that only superficially describe its appearance in practice. Due to the Administrative Organisation Law, jurisprudential knowledge of state regulation and the economic approaches of the New Institutional Economics can be related methodologically.[17] Thus, the influence of organisations on decisions of the banking regulation is examined with the aid of approaches from the Institutional Economics. Organisations are all national public regulators, European associations of public regulators and plural regulation actors. They pursue the regulation of markets to secure the common good. The organisation of the actors is done by the appropriate configuration of institutions.[18] Institutions are formal and informal rules (norms); combined they form a system through which the behaviour of organisations can be controlled.[19] The economic concept of institutions means the legal

---

[14]In detail Höfling, Gutachten zum 68. Deutschen Juristentag, (C.H. Beck, 2010), F43 et seq.

[15]Schmidt-Aßmann, Einführung, in Schmidt-Aßmann and Hoffmann-Riem (Eds.), Verwaltungsorganisationsrecht als Steuerungsressource, (Nomos, 1997), 9 (20).

[16]Schuppert, Verwaltungswissenschaft, (Nomos, 2000), 547; Weaver and Rockman, Assessing the effects of institutions, When and how do institutions matter, in Weaver and Rockman (Eds.), Do Institutions matter? Government Capabilities in the United States and Abroad, (Brookings Institute, 1993), 1 (9).

[17]Möllers, Der vermisste Leviathan, (Suhrkamp, 2008), 83; Ruffert, Begriff, in Fehling and Ruffert (Eds.), Regulierungsrecht, (Mohr Siebeck, 2010), § 7 paras. 18, 22.

[18]Erlei, Leschke and Sauerland, Neue Institutionenökonomik, 2nd ed. (Schäffer-Poeschel, 2007), 22, 65; Richter and Furobotn, Neue Institutionenökonomik, 4th ed. (Mohr Siebeck, 2010), 7 et seq.

[19]North, Institutions, institutional change and economic performance, (Cambridge University Press, 1991), 3 et seq.; Leschke, Regulierungstheorie aus ökonomischer Sicht, in Fehling and Ruffert (Eds.), Regulierungsrecht, (Mohr Siebeck, 2010), § 6 para. 13.

bases (including laws, regulations, contracts, rules of procedures) of players in the banking regulation. They determine who is responsible for decisions in a particular area and which procedures need to be followed.[20] *Douglass C. North* establishes a link between organisation and institution, after which the development of the organisation depends on institutional frameworks, while organisations themselves affect the development of the institutional framework.[21]

The regulation of financial institutions is based on uncertainties, since the business of the financial sector has to deal with risks which may affect private investors and the economy as a whole. Aim of the banking regulation is both, to reduce information asymmetries between banks as providers and private clients as buyers, and to generate confidence in the financial market. Particularly, economic uncertainties are difficult to regulate. Which institutions are considered systemically relevant? How much capital is needed to cover the risk? What minimum liquidity is required to ensure the solvency of credit institutions? The administration of regulation requires comprehensive information to reduce factual uncertainties[22] in the banking regulation. This dilemma is less resolved through a substantive and procedural programme control as through the institutional arrangements of the organisations that programme methods and control decisions.

### *1.1.3 Overview of the Legal Basis of Banking Regulation*

Terminologically this study deals with the administrative organisation of banking regulation. The focus is set on all administrative actors who are entrusted with the supervision, recovery and management of financial institutions. The rules made for the supervision and the rules made for the recovery and resolution of financial institutions deserve special attention. Fundamental impulses emerged at an international level. These impulses embraced directives and regulations at a European level before they were transposed in national law or were applied directly.

With the Declaration on Strengthening the Financial System[23] of the Heads of State and Government (Group of Twenty in April 2009), the Financial Stability Board was established. The board was, among other things, given the tasks to evaluate the stability of the global financial system, to identify systemically important and cross-border financial institutions, and to promote the cooperation

[20]Arrow, Essays in the theory of risk-bearing, (North-Holland Publications, 1971), 224 et seq.

[21]North, Institutions, institutional change and economic performance, (Cambridge University Press, 1991), 5, 8.

[22]Knight, Risk, Uncertainty and Profit, (Harper & Row, 1971), 259 et seq.; for more details about generating knowledge as problem of regulation see Herzmann, Konsultationen, (Mohr Siebeck, 2010), 33 et seq.

[23]G20 Declaration on Strengthening the Financial System, London Summit, 2 April 2009 (available online, last downloaded 28.02.2015 at http://www.g20ys.org/upload/files/London_2.pdf).

and exchange of information between the Financial Supervisory Authorities to implement regulatory and supervisory measures.

These regulations were supplemented by the Basel Committee on Banking Supervision with the framework "Basel III: A global regulatory framework for more resilient banks and banking systems"[24] to strengthen the quality and quantity of equity, broader securitisation of risks with equity, international liquidity and risk management standards and to supervise systemically relevant banks.[25] Geographical disadvantages of financial centres can be avoided by worldwide standard rules. The financial crisis has revealed discrepancies between different national regulatory rules and surveillance actors in Europe.[26] Fragmented supervisory rules and competences could not be properly coordinated during the crisis.[27] There is a tension between government requirements for the provision of equity capital and a fair, private competition in the European internal market.[28] Goals of a fundamental reform of the financial regulation were detailed substantive and procedural programmes and extensive regulation *actors* to submit the financial industry to stricter regulation. At the same time, the legislative techniques of the European Union changed its course. Substantive and procedural requirements of the banking regulation were regulated according to Art 288 (3) Treaty on the Functioning of the European Union (TFEU)[29] by means of directives that were only binding as to the result to be achieved. Member States were left with the choice of form and method. So the national legislators remained with a little scope for implementation. Under the impact of the financial crisis, a group of experts, under the direction of former International Monetary Fund (IMF) president Jacques de Larosière, came to the conclusion that the national scope of implementation led to an inconsistent European regulatory framework.[30] Instead, regulation was recommended as instrument to avoid such scopes in the future.[31] The interaction of directive and regulation was supposed to create a high level of harmonisation in the banking regulation. Therewith, regulatory forbearance through the Member States and regulatory

---

[24]Bank for International Settlements, A global regulatory framework for more resilient banks and banking systems 2010; revised version published in June 2011 (available online, last downloaded 28.02.2015 at: http://www.bis.org/publ/bcbs189.pdf).

[25]For further details see Bundesbankpublikation: Basel III – Leitfaden zu den neuen Eigenkapital und Liquiditätsregeln für Banken, (Deutsche Bundesbank, 2011).

[26]Wymeersch, The new European financial regulatory bodies, revue bancaire et financière (2012), 28 (29).

[27]Ferber, Die Neuordnung der Europäischen Aufsichtsstruktur, Ifo-Schnelldienst 64 (2011), 9 (10).

[28]Schäfer/Rolker, Bankenaufsicht im Spannungsfeld von Regulierung und Wettbewerb, in Grieser and Heemann (Eds.), Bankenaufsicht nach der Finanzmarktkrise, (Frankfurt School Verlag, 2011), 3 (9).

[29]Consolidated version of the Treaty on the Functioning of the European Union, OJ C 326, 26.10.2012, p. 47.

[30]De Larosière Report, 25 February 2009, paras.99, 102 (available online, last downloaded 28.02.2015 at: http://ec.europa.eu/internal_market/finances/docs/de_larosiere_report_en.pdf).

[31]De Larosière Report, 25 February 2009, para.110 (available online, last downloaded 28.02.2015 at: http://ec.europa.eu/internal_market/finances/docs/de_larosiere_report_en.pdf).

capture between national supervisory boards and financial institutions were supposed to be avoided.[32] As result the substantive provisions of the Basel III framework were implemented through the Capital Requirements Directive IV[33] and the Capital Requirements Regulation[34] in the European Union.[35] In addition, the European Commission adopted regulatory technical and implementing standards, developed by the European Banking Authority. Under the heading "Single Rule Book" supervisory rules were ought to extend themselves not only to large credit institutes (as planned in Basel III), but also to all credit institutes and investment firms.

Furthermore, the Financial Stability Board designed "Key Attributes of Effective Resolution Regime for Financial Institutions"[36] at an international level. This impetus was implemented at a European level by the Directive establishing a framework for the recovery and resolution of credit institutions and investment firms,[37] which creates a material framework that harmonises the recovery and resolution instruments. In addition, the Regulation establishing uniform rules and a uniform procedure[38] complements the already advanced stage of the development of a uniform European monitoring mechanism.[39] The goal is to provide tools, which enable a bank resolution without using the taxpayers' money.

The Federal Republic of Germany implemented the market-related Regulation in accordance with the German Securities Trading Act[40] and the institutional

[32]Kämmerer, Bahn frei der Bankenunion, Neue Zeitschrift für Verwaltungsrecht (2013), 830 (831).

[33]Directive 2013/36/EU of the European Parliament and of the Council of 26 June 2013 on access to the activity of credit institutions and the prudential supervision of credit institutions and investment firms, OJ L 176, 27.06.2013, p.338.

[34]Regulation (EU) No 575/2013 of the European Parliament and of the Council of 26 June 2013 on prudential requirements for credit institutions and investment firms, OJ L 321, 30.11.2013, p.6.

[35]For further details see Höpfner, CRD IV Regulierungspaket für Banken, BaFin Journal 1/2014, 21 et seq.

[36]Financial Stability Board, Key Attributes of Effective Resolution Regimes for Financial Institutions, 2011, updated version published October 2014 (available online, last downloaded 28.02.2015 at: http://www.financialstabilityboard.org/wp-content/uploads/r_141015.pdf).

[37]Directive 2014/59/EU of the European Parliament and of the Council of 15 May 2014 establishing a framework for the recovery and resolution of credit institutions and investment firms, OJ L 173, 12.06.2014, p.190.

[38]Regulation (EU) No 806/2014 of the European Parliament and of the Council of 15 July 2014 establishing uniform rules and a uniform procedure for the resolution of credit institutions and certain investment firms in the framework of a Single Resolution Mechanism and a Single Resolution Fund, OJ L 225, 30.07.2014, p.1.

[39]In detail Zimmer, Gutachten zum 68. Deutschen Juristentag, (C.H. Beck, 2010), G 49 et seq.

[40]Gesetz über den Wertpapierhandel (Wertpapierhandelsgesetz – WpHG) as published in the announcement of 09 April 1998 (Federal Law Gazette I, p. 2708), last amended on 15 July 2014 (Federal Law Gazette I, p. 934).

supervision in accordance with the German Banking Act.[41] This is, in terms of recovery and resolution, by the Restructuring Act[42] and—recently announced—the Recovery and Resolution Act [43] coming into force as of 01.01.2015. Formally, the ongoing supervision is performed by the Deutsche Bundesbank, while the German Federal Financial Supervisory Authority shall make supervisory decisions and the Agency for Financial Stability carries out the recovery and regulation of credit institutes.

### *1.1.4 State of Previous Investigations*

A study on the legal assessment of the impact of organisations on decision-making in bank Regulation Law does not exist. The Administrative Organisation Law and approaches of the New Institutional Economics are ought to serve as model for this study.

The research on the influence of organisations on decision-making focuses on socio-economic studies on the use of uncertainties while making decisions. The political scientists Dorothea Jansen and Klaus Schubert raise the question "how interactions and constellations of actors influence the result." In terms of New Institutional Economics authors to mention are Douglass C. North and Kenneth J. Arrow. Arrow examines an "interest in studying how organisations solve their problems". North emphasises that "organisations [...] will reflect the opportunities provided by the institutional matrix" as a "fundamental long-run source of change". The legal research does not go beyond first attempts. [44] Only William E. Kovacic uses the example of a competition law from an Anglo-American perspective and establishes that "institutional considerations are beginning to receive the attention they deserve".[45] A coherent doctrine has not yet developed.

Particularly, the field of Regulation Law, in which organisations clearly define and carry out the substantive law requirements, the relationship between organisation and decision-making in the German and European law is only discussed

[41]Gesetz über das Kreditwesen (Kreditwesengesetz – KWG) as published in the announcement of 09. September 1998 (Federal Law Gazette I, p. 2776) last amended on 15 July 2014 (Federal Law Gazette I, p. 934).

[42]Gesetz zur Reorganisation von Kreditinstituten (Kreditinstitute-Reorganisationsgesetz – KredReorgG) as published in the announcement of 09. December 2010 (Federal Law Gazette I, p. 1900) last amended on 22 December 2011 (Federal Law Gazette I, p. 3044).

[43]Gesetz zur Sanierung und Abwicklung von Instituten und Finanzgruppen (Sanierungs- und Abwicklungsgesetz – SAG) as published in the announcement of 10 Dezember 2014 (Federal Law Gazette I, p. 2091).

[44]Posner, Economic Analysis of Law, 8th ed. (Wolters Kluwer International, 2011), 31, 33.

[45]Kovacic, Distinguished essay: Good agency practice and the implementation of competition law, in Hermann, Krajewski and Terhechte (Eds.), European Yearbook of International Economic Law, Vol. 4 (2013), 3 (6).

basically. Trends in legal literature tend to describe the organisational forms of banking regulation without discussing their influence on regulatory decisions. Based on these descriptions, the given problem can be viewed systematically.

Given the high practical relevance of the legal assessment of the relationship between organisational forms and decisions in the banking regulation, it appears to be essential to systematically classify and link the multitude of regulatory actors.

## 1.2 Aim of the Investigation

This study aims to determine the organisation of the administration of regulation in the European Composite Administration at a national, European and international level. Therefore, organisational models are created. In addition, a focus is set on two frameworks: on the one hand, on the legal basis for the organisation of banking regulation and, on the other hand, on the dilemma between monetary policy and banking regulation with regard to regulatory decisions.

Centre of investigation is the question how organisational forms influence decision-making in the banking regulation. Associated with this is the question how the administration of regulation can close the gap between the given and needed information. Given information are already owned or can be gained by the administration of regulation. Information not given but needed is important to know to adequately regulate the markets. This work starts on the administrative organisation of the administration of regulation in the reference area of banking regulation. There are different institutional requirements for equipping organisations. These organisations can generate knowledge and participate in the regulatory decision-making process. Thus, each organisation form has a different influence on decision-making in the European regulatory network. This allows the organisation of banking regulation to serve as a basis for discussions in the regulatory practice.

The aim of the investigation is to come up with theses for the organisation of the administration of regulation to meet the dynamic conditions of the financial sector by organised regulatory actors. The resulting theses can be viewed from two different angles. From one perspective, the effect of different institutional arrangements for the organisational design can be derived. From the other perspective, constructive approaches can be gained by creating models to develop or reform the administration of regulation in other economic sectors.

The investigation will in particular show that the density of regulation within the institutional framework affects the organisational power of the regulatory actors, and that the organisational power is correlated with the influence of regulatory actors on the decision-making process.

## 1.3 Course of Investigation

The investigation of the relationship of organisation and decision on the example of banking regulation calls for a terminological introduction. Approaching the concepts of administration and organisation enables to work out key elements of the administrative organisation design, which are used in the following to create administrative organisations in the banking regulation. Subsequently, the concept of regulation is defined in the broader sense of the word as used in financial markets and financial institutions. Thus, the functions of banking regulation can be understood. Against the background of this abstract introduction, the unique challenges of banking regulation are outlined. These challenges comprise asymmetric information, actual uncertainties and incomplete knowledge.

Five model types of administrative organisations are set up, based on administrative organisation elements. Particular importance is placed on the institutional arrangements of the organisation, as they define the principles, competencies and relationships between the respective actors. Then, the manifestations of the administration of regulation are classified with a total of eleven actors in an organisational and process sequence of banking regulation. Following this, the organisation models and their respective manifestations in banking regulation are placed in a matrix of institutional organisational power and their respective influence on regulatory decision.

Seven theses on the organisation of banking regulation derive from the systematic analysis of banking regulation actors: the organisation of banking regulation follows no legal foundation in the European Treaties (I), the banking supervision by the European Central Bank (ECB) is incompatible with their contractual mandate for monetary policy (II), the European bank resolution leads to a communitarisation of liability (III), the European banking regulation is incompatible with the determination of the German Basic Law for democratic legitimacy (IV), banking supervision collides with the model of the Union law enforcement (V), the density of regulation of the institutional framework affects the organisational power of the regulatory actors (VI), the organisational power correlates with the influence of regulatory actors on decisions (VII).

Finally, a summary on the organisation of banking regulation is given.

# Chapter 2
# Administrative Organisation of Banking Regulation

## 2.1 The Concept of Administrative Organisation

Administrative Organisation and Administrative Organisation Law are mostly described at an abstract level in administrative science.[1] This is because the dogmatic foundations, developed in earlier times, of the German Federal and Union Administration have not been adjusted in accordance with the ongoing developments and various phenomena of administrative reality. As a result, the administrative organisation is exhausted in a variety of exceptions in regard to a lack of consistent systematic rules.

An approach to the concept of administrative organisation should take place by means of a not only semantic separation of the concepts of administration and organisation in order to identify the elements of administrative organisation and their interplay (Sect. 2.1). Based on this, the functions of administrative organisation used for controlling administrative action can be understood (Sect. 2.2). Although the forms of administrative organisation differ at a national and European level, as well as in different areas of administration between state and society, administrative organisations have common elements (Sect. 2.3). They form the conceptual basis for the following analysis of banking regulation.

### 2.1.1 *Organising Administration*

A first approach to the concept of "administration" can be derived from the meaning of the word itself. "Administer" means as much as "to affect something",

---

The conception of this chapter and the main reasoning is based on broader explanations in Chapter 2 in Wellerdt, Organisation der Regulierungsverwaltung, forthcoming.

[1]Schmidt-Aßmann, Das allgemeine Verwaltungsrecht als Ordnungsidee, 2nd ed. (Springer, 2004), Ch. 5. para. 2; Groß, Das Kollegialprinzip in der Verwaltungsorganisation, (Mohr Siebeck, 1999), 8 et seq.



A. Wellerdt, *Organisation of Banking Regulation*, SpringerBriefs in Law,
DOI 10.1007/978-3-319-17638-3_2

"to manage something", and "to direct the taking of something".[2] In addition, a holistic definition of the term "administration" has not been accepted until today.[3] The reason lies in the nature of administration, as it is possible to describe but not define administration.[4] Administration needs to be open for further developments to deal with new manifestations in economics and society. This means: administration is the sum of all state bodies involved in the performance of public services.[5]

In addition, administration has not only a substantive executive, but also a formally organising function.[6] The concept of administration is understood and used ambiguously. Administration describes diverse, purposive performances of duties for the common good by trustees appointed for this purpose. Further, administration describes the entirety of bodies of the nation-state and supranational organisations, which administer social and economic areas. Administration is a system supporting the decision-making process.

It processes stimuli from the environment, in order to carry out administrative tasks and to fulfil administrative purposes.[7] Hence, administration describes, on the one hand, a dynamic, multi-functional activity of administering different areas of life and economy. On the other hand, it is understood as a synonym for the static organisation of performing state activities.[8] With that, administration is an organisational unit which organises state action.

---

[2]Duden Band 10 – Das Bedeutungswörterbuch, 4th ed. (Bibliographisches Institut, 2010), 1045, 1045; Stober, in Wolff, Bachof, Stober and Kluth (Eds.), Verwaltungsrecht I, 12th ed. (C.H. Beck, 2007), § 3 para. 8 et seq.; Ellwein, Einführung in die Regierungs- und Verwaltungslehre, (Kohlhammer, 1966), 108 et seq.

[3]Forsthoff, Lehrbuch des Verwaltungsrechts, Erster Band: Allgemeiner Teil, 10th ed. (C.H. Beck, 1973), § 1 I: "Von jeher ist die Verwaltungsrechtswissenschaft um eine Definition ihres Gegenstandes, der Verwaltung, verlegen"; this view is supported by Stober, in Wolff, Bachof, Stober and Kluth (Eds.), Verwaltungsrecht I, 12th ed. (C.H. Beck 2007), § 3 para. 3; Möllers, Gewaltengliederung, (Mohr Siebeck, 2006), 112 et seq.

[4]Forsthoff, Lehrbuch des Verwaltungsrechts, Erster Band: Allgemeiner Teil, 10th ed. (C.H. Beck, 1973), § 1 I.

[5]Püttner, Verwaltungslehre, 4th ed. (C.H. Beck, 2007), § 4 I para. 10; Moreover, the positive concepts take up different, typical features of the administration, instead of many Ehlers, Staatliche Verwaltung, in Erichsen and Ehlers (Eds.), Allgemeines Verwaltungsrecht, 14th ed. (De Gruyter, 2010), § 1 para. 6 with other references in footnotes 8-21.

[6]Thieme, Verwaltungslehre, (Carl Heymanns, 1984), § 1 paras. 5 et seq.; Groß, Die Verwaltungsorganisation als Teil organisierter Staatlichkeit, in Hoffmann-Riem, Schmidt-Aßmann and Voßkuhle (Eds.), Grundlagen des Verwaltungsrechts – Vol.1, 2nd ed. (C.H. Beck, 2012), § 13 para. 7, Bull and Mehde (Eds.), Allgemeines Verwaltungsrecht, 8th ed. (C.F. Müller, 2009), § 10 para. 371; Möllers, Gewaltengliederung, (Mohr Siebeck, 2006), 114, 117.

[7]Krebs, Die Juristische Methode im Verwaltungsrecht, in Schmidt-Aßmann and Hoffmann-Riem (Eds.), Methoden der Verwaltungsrechtswissenschaft, (Nomos, 2004), 209; for basic understanding Trute, Methodik der Herstellung und Darstellung verwaltungsrechtlicher Entscheidungen, in Schmidt-Aßmann and Hoffmann-Riem (Eds.), Methoden der Verwaltungsrechtswissenschaft, (Nomos, 2004), 293 (306 et seq.).

[8]Krebs, Verwaltungsorganisation, in Isensee and Kirchhof (Eds.), Handbuch des Staatsrechts – Vol. V, 3rd ed. (C.F. Müller, 2007), § 108 para. 1; Thieme, Verwaltungslehre, (Carl Heymanns, 1984), § 1 para. 9; Schuppert, Verwaltungswissenschaft, (Nomos, 2000), 79 et seq.

## 2.1.2 Administering Organisation

A definition of the concept "Organisation" has already taken place in economics,[9] social sciences[10] and jurisprudence.[11] Thus, the concept of organisation is ambiguous because of its different meanings. Its meanings range from the organising process over the internal order of an administrative unit up to the social structure as such.[12]

Organisations are complex social structures that work under the principle of job-sharing. From the outside they appear as an integrated whole.[13] They rather combine interrelated actions and communications within or between administrative units.[14] Organisations administer actions and communications by performing duties in a strict hierarchical or collegial[15] order. These duties are assigned to specialised organisation members with the help of a detailed programming.[16]

Like the concept of administration, the concept of organisation is understood equivocal.[17] An organisation describes not only institutionally a static unit of bodies.

---

[9]Kosiol, Organisation der Unternehmung, 2nd ed. (Gabler, 1976),15 et seq.; 186 et seq.; Wöhe and Döring, Einführung in die allgemeine Betriebswirtschaftslehre, 25th ed. (Vahlen, 2013), 100 et seq.

[10]Luhmann, Funktionen und Folgen formaler Organisation, 2nd ed. (Duncker & Humblot, 1972), 29, 31 et seq.; Mayntz, Soziologie der öffentlichen Verwaltung, (C.F.Müller, 1978), 82 et seq.

[11]Kluth, in Wolff, Bachof, Stober and Kluth (Eds.), Verwaltungsrecht II, 7th ed. (C.H. Beck, 2010), § 79 I paras. 3 et seq.; Burgi, Verwaltungsorganisationsrecht, in Erichsen and Ehlers (Eds.), Allgemeines Verwaltungsrecht, 14th ed. (De Gruyter, 2010), § 7 paras. 4 et seq., for further details see Schuppert, Verwaltungswissenschaft – Verwaltung, Verwaltungsrecht, Verwaltungslehre, (Nomos, 2000).

[12]Cf. Krebs, Verwaltungsorganisation, in Isensee and Kirchhof (Eds.), Handbuch des Staatsrechts – Vol. V, 3rd ed. (C.F. Müller, 2007), § 108 para. 2; Mayntz, Soziologie der Organisation, (Rowohlt, 1963), 36 et seq.; Kosiol, Organisation der Unternehmung, 2nd ed. (Gabler, 1976), 15 et seq.; 19 et seq.

[13]Schmidt-Aßmann, Einführung, in Schmidt-Aßmann and Hoffmann-Riem (Eds.), Verwaltungsorganisationsrecht als Steuerungsressource, (Nomos, 1997), 11 (34); Kluth, in Wolff, Bachof, Stober and Kluth (Eds.), Verwaltungsrecht II, 7th ed. (C.H. Beck, 2010), § 79 I paras. 13 et seq.; Schuppert, Verwaltungswissenschaft, (Nomos, 2000), 767 et seq.; Luhmann, Funktionen und Folgen formaler Organisation, 2nd ed. (Duncker & Humblot, 1972), 23 et seq.

[14]Schmidt-Aßmann, Einführung, in Schmidt-Aßmann and Hoffmann-Riem (Eds.), Verwaltungsorganisationsrecht als Steuerungsressource, (Nomos, 1997), 11 (34); Trute, Die Funktionen von Organisationen und ihre Abbildung im Recht, in Schmidt-Aßmann and Hoffmann-Riem (Eds.), Verwaltungsorganisationsrecht als Steuerungsressource, (Nomos, 1997), 249 (254, 263 et seq.); Brohm, Strukturen der Wirtschaftsverwaltung, (Kohlhammer, 1969), 16 et seq.

[15]Groß, Das Kollegialprinzip in der Verwaltungsorganisation, (Mohr Siebeck, 1999), 111 et seq.

[16]Groß, Grundzüge der organisationswissenschaftlichen Diskussion, in Schmidt-Aßmann and Hoffmann-Riem (Eds.), Verwaltungsorganisationsrecht als Steuerungsressource, (Nomos, 1997), 139 (141).

[17]Schmidt-Aßmann, Einführung, in Schmidt-Aßmann and Hoffmann-Riem (Eds.), Verwaltungsorganisationsrecht als Steuerungsressource, (Nomos, 1997), 11 (35); Groß, Die Verwaltungsorganisation als Teil organisierter Staatlichkeit, in Hoffmann-Riem, Schmidt-Aßmann and Voßkuhle (Eds.), Grundlagen des Verwaltungsrechts – Vol.1, 2nd ed. (C.H. Beck, 2012) § 13 para. 4.

An organisation was created as a dynamic organising instrument for the fulfilment of tasks. It takes action to guide administrative actions in a certain direction.[18] Thus, the organisation creates an institutional framework for the decision-making process and it further enriches it with administration decisions.[19] In other words, organisation is the appearance and realisation of administration.[20]

### 2.1.3 Meaning of Administrative Organisation

The rules of the administrative organisation of national and European administrative bodies arise especially through laws, regulations or statutes and through frameworks of the German Basic Law[21] or the Treaty on the Functioning of the European Union with its principles of democracy and rule of law.

Administrative organisation is the best possible fulfilment of public services.[22] They possess and link elementary functions.[23] First, administrative organisations can reduce possible decision uncertainties by collecting and comparing the organisation's own knowledge. Furthermore, they can flexibly combine resources of all organisation members, generate information, learn from practical experiences and gain new knowledge.[24]

The administrative organisation constitutes the 'structural requirements of administering'[25] in two respects: first, the structure of the administrative organisation determines the administrative action and second, structured administrative

---

[18]Groß, Das Kollegialprinzip in der Verwaltungsorganisation, (Mohr Siebeck, 1999), 11, 19; for more details see Ellwein, Regieren und Verwalten (Westdeutscher Verlag, 1976), 148.

[19]Groß, Das Kollegialprinzip in der Verwaltungsorganisation, (Mohr Siebeck, 1999) 19 et seq.; Kluth, in Wolff, Bachof, Stober and Kluth (Eds.), 7th ed. (C.H. Beck, 2010), § 79 II paras. 1, 93.

[20]Krebs, Verwaltungsorganisation, in Isensee and Kirchhof (Eds.), Handbuch des Staatsrechts – Vol. V, 3rd ed. (C.F. Müller, 2007), § 108 para. 1.

[21]Grundgesetz für die Bundesrepublik Deutschland in the revised version published in the Federal Law Gazette Part III, number 100-1, as last amended on 23.12.2014 (Federal Law Gazette I p. 2438).

[22]Püttner, Verwaltungslehre, 4th ed. (C.H. Beck, 2007), § 7 I para. 1; Loeser, System des Verwaltungsrechts – Vol 2, (Nomos, 1994), § 10 para. 1.

[23]Schmidt-Aßmann, Einführung, in Schmidt-Aßmann and Hoffmann-Riem (Eds.), Verwaltungsorganisationsrecht als Steuerungsressource, (Nomos, 1997), 11 (19).

[24]Eifert, Innovation in und durch Netzwerkorganisation: Relevanz, Regulierung und staatliche Einbindung, in Eifert and Hoffmann-Riem (Eds.), Innovation und rechtliche Regulierung, (Nomos, 2002), 88 (95 et seq.); Schuppert, Verwaltungsorganisation und Verwaltungsorganisationsrecht als Steuerungsfaktoren, in Hoffmann-Riem, Schmidt-Aßmann and Voßkuhle (Eds.), Grundlagen des Verwaltungsrechts – Vol.1, 2nd ed. (C.H. Beck, 2012) § 16 paras. 139 et seq.

[25]Schuppert, Verwaltungsrechtswissenschaft als Steuerungswissenschaft. Zur Steuerung des Verwaltungshandelns durch Verwaltungsrecht, in Schmidt-Aßmann, Hoffmann-Riem and Schuppert (Eds.), Zur Reform des Allgemeinen Verwaltungsrechts, (Nomos, 1993), 67 et seq.; Schmidt-Aßmann, Einführung, in Schmidt-Aßmann and Hoffmann-Riem (Eds.), Verwaltungsorganisationsrecht als Steuerungsressource, (Nomos, 1997), 9 (20).

actions require an adequate administrative organisation. So, administrative organisations give static and structure to administration units and have a dynamic structuring effect on administrative action. Thus, administrative organisation gains not only formally, but also materially importance for the control of administrative decisions. This interdependency enables a special form of control. The concept of control is terminologically described as a *structure management*[26] or *controlling organisation.*[27] Behind these conceptualisations stands the realisation that the Administrative Organisation Law creates structures in which functions, relationships and decisions are organisationally and coherently controlled. In the following analysis, administrative organisation is seen as a medium that controls the decision-making process of the administration through a legal structuring of the organisation.

## 2.2 Functions of the Administrative Organisation

Administrative organisation has a double function.[28] It determines structures and creates the structures of the administrative organisation.

### *2.2.1 Constitution and Control*

The administrative organisation plays an institutional function by regulating the internal organisation and external relations of independent administrative units.[29]

[26] Schuppert, Verwaltungsorganisation und Verwaltungsorganisationsrecht als Steuerungsfaktoren, in Hoffmann-Riem, Schmidt-Aßmann and Voßkuhle (Eds.), Grundlagen des Verwaltungsrechts – Vol.1, 2nd ed. (C.H. Beck, 2012) § 16 paras.10, 19.

[27] Schmidt-Aßmann, Einführung, in Schmidt-Aßmann and Hoffmann-Riem (Eds.), Verwaltungsorganisationsrecht als Steuerungsressource, (Nomos, 1997), 11(14); Schmidt-Aßmann, Das allgemeine Verwaltungsrecht als Ordnungsidee, 2nd ed. (Springer 2004), Ch. 5 paras. 9 et seq.

[28] Schmidt-Aßmann, Das allgemeine Verwaltungsrecht als Ordnungsidee, 2nd ed. (Springer 2004), Ch. 5 para. 1; Schmidt-Aßmann, Einführung, in Schmidt-Aßmann and Hoffmann-Riem (Eds.), Verwaltungsorganisationsrecht als Steuerungsressource, (Nomos, 1997), 11 (11, 19 et seq.); Groß, Das Kollegialprinzip in der Verwaltungsorganisation, (Mohr Siebeck, 1999), 10 et seq.; for different opinions see Schuppert, Verwaltungsorganisation und Verwaltungsorganisationsrecht als Steuerungsfaktoren, in Hoffmann-Riem, Schmidt-Aßmann and Voßkuhle (Eds.), Grundlagen des Verwaltungsrechts – Vol.1, 2nd ed. (C.H. Beck, 2012), § 16 paras. 2 et seq. Who thinks about three functions (function of constitution, function of control, democratic function) and Loeser, System des Verwaltungsrechts – Vol. II, (Nomos, 1994), § 10 paras. 10 et seq. Who thinks about four functions (function of the rule of law, realisation of fundamental rights through organisation, democratic function, transmission function through the implementation of fundamental values and structures).

[29] Schuppert, Verwaltungsorganisation und Verwaltungsorganisationsrecht als Steuerungsfaktoren, in Hoffmann-Riem, Schmidt-Aßmann and Voßkuhle (Eds.), Grundlagen des Verwaltungsrechts – Vol.1, 2nd ed. (C.H. Beck, 2012), § 16 paras. 8; 19; Schmidt-Aßmann, Das allgemeine Verwaltungsrecht als Ordnungsidee, 2nd ed. (Springer, 2004), Ch. 1. para. 36; Groß, Das Kollegialprinzip in der Verwaltungsorganisation, (Mohr Siebeck, 1999), 18 et seq.

On this institutional basis the administrative organisation develops its instrumental function. It allows the control of administrative decisions by assigning tasks and decision-making powers. Put simply, the constitution of the administrative organisation creates a framework for controlling administrative actions.

First, the administrative organisation processes dynamically stimuli from its environment. Then, the control is oriented towards the specific goals of the static administrative organisation, resulting from particular tasks that have to be performed.[30] Main objective of the administrative organisation is always the realisation of the substantive law.[31]

### 2.2.2 Meaning of the Administrative Organisation Law

The administrative organisation is determined by the Administrative Organisation Law.[32] It gives a normative basis to the administrative organisation. It establishes the constitution of an organisation and regulates the connection and the functioning of the bodies in the administrative apparatus. Thus, the regulatory effect of the Administrative Organisation Law has an "ambiguity" towards the inside and the outside.[33] Special importance is gained by the Administrative Organisation Law by the involvement of national and unional administrations in the European Composite Administration.[34] This serves the task-related control of the Union's own administration, the national government administrations and the inter-national state administrative cooperation.[35] In this framework, the Administrative Organisation Law structures the systemic forces and balances the interactions between actors. With that, organisations and proceedings become important control resources in an

---

[30]Trute, Methodik der Herstellung und Darstellung verwaltungsrechtlicher Entscheidungen, in Schmidt-Aßmann and Hoffmann-Riem (Eds.), Methoden der Verwaltungswissenschaft, (Nomos, 2004), 249 (257 et seq.); Burgi, Verwaltungsorganisationsrecht, in Erichsen and Ehlers (Eds.), Allgemeines Verwaltungsrecht, 14th ed. (De Gruyter, 2010), § 7 para. 14.

[31]Burgi, Verwaltungsorganisationsrecht, in Erichsen and Ehlers (Eds.), Allgemeines Verwaltungsrecht, 14th ed. (De Gruyter, 2010), § 7 para. 15; Loeser, System des Verwaltungsrechts – Vol.II, (Nomos, 1994), § 10 paras. 2 et seq.

[32]Möllers, Materielles Recht – Verfahrensrecht – Organisationsrecht, in Trute, Groß, Röhl and Möllers (Eds.), Allgemeines Verwaltungsrecht – zur Tragfähigkeit eines Konzepts, (Mohr Siebeck, 2008), 489 (500).

[33]Brohm, Strukturen der Wirtschaftsverwaltung, (Kohlhammer, 1969), 18.

[34]Coining of the term, see Schmidt-Aßmann, Einleitung: Der Europäische Verwaltungsverbund und die Rolle des europäischen Verwaltungsrechts, in Schmidt-Aßmann and Schöndorf-Haubold (Eds.), Der Europäische Verwaltungsverbund, (Mohr Siebeck, 2005), 1 (7 et seq.).

[35]For elementary information see Schmidt-Aßmann, Die Herausforderung der Verwaltungswissenschaft durch die Internationalisierung der Verwaltungsbeziehungen, Der Staat 45 (2006), 315 et seq.

independent political and economic context.[36] Central importance is attributed to the administrative organisation as a framework and resource for controlling the decision-making process.

## 2.3 Elements of the Administrative Organisation Design

Because public services, policies and institutional frameworks are too different, administration and administrative organisation do not form a uniformly structured entity.[37] Hence, it is not possible to structure and standardise the entire administration. Nevertheless, depending on the administrative unit, there are elements of the administrative organisation that influence administrative actions. Administrative science brought out a number of administrative organisations features that are linked in this study and also used as basis for a concrete modelling. For this purpose, a first localisation of elements of organisation is done in the reference field of banking regulation.

### *2.3.1 Legal Form of the Organisation*

The most important task of the administrative organisation is to find a legal form for the organisation. The legal form sets the outer frame of the organisation and influences its action. Its justification may lie in different acts of law for example from law to regulation to statutes up to concrete and general agreements. The legal form of the organisation determines which impetuses are picked up and which instruments are chosen to process the stimulus. It also characterises the meaning and the function of the administrative organisation in the Composite Administration. Furthermore, it lays down the legal status of the organisation as well as its legal capacity and its capacity to act. The legal capacity affects the relationship of the organisation and other organisations. The capacity to act affects the performance of public services and the legal quality of the organisational action.

Within the banking regulation there are eleven representative administration units at national, European and international level that contribute to the regulation

[36]Schmidt-Aßmann, Europäische Verwaltung zwischen Kooperation und Hierarchie, in Cremer, Giegerich, Richter and Zimmermann (Eds.), Festschrift für Helmut Steinberger, (Springer, 2002), 1375 (1390 et seq.; 1399); deepening Schmidt-Aßmann, Einleitung: Der Europäische Verwaltungsverbund und die Rolle des europäischen Verwaltungsrechts, in Schmidt-Aßmann and Schöndorf-Haubold (Eds.), Der Europäische Verwaltungsverbund, (Mohr Siebeck, 2005), 1 (22 et seq.); Ruffert transfers and extends this approach also on the international administrative law, Perspektiven des Internationalen Verwaltungsrechts, in Möllers, Voßkuhle and Walter (Eds.), Internationales Verwaltungsrecht, (Mohr Siebeck, 2007), 395 (405).

[37]Püttner, Verwaltungslehre, 4th ed. (C.H. Beck, 2007), § 7 para. 1.

of credit institutions. The multitude of actors reflects also the variety of legal forms of organisations. In addition to legally constituted national authorities or the European agencies with certain competences and instruments, also influential committees and bodies have been formed. They especially act on the international scene and only have vaguely determinable capacity to act due to a lack of a concrete legal basis.

## *2.3.2 Institutions of the Organisation*

Institutions of the organisation are an element of the organisational design, imported from the New Institutional Economics. The New Institutional Economics pursues two approaches that are usable for a jurisprudential analysis.

First, the New Institutional Economics examines the importance of institutions for a company's economic behaviour. The results can be transferred to the administrative actions of administrative organisations. Moreover, the "transaction costs"[38] resulting from seeking information, negotiations and enforcement of decisions can be projected on administrative units to control decision-making processes in administrative organisations.[39] The medium to create an appropriate organisational structure and to control decision-making are so called institutions.[40] Institutions describe a set of rules that determine the administrative structure and programme the administrative pattern to reduce transaction costs.[41] Within these structures, individual decisions are developed and carried out depending on type and scope.[42] Finally, the New Institutional Economics recognises a link between organisation and institution, after which the development of the organisation depends on the institutional framework. Organisations on the other hand affect the development of the institutional framework.[43]

---

[38]Coase, The Problem of Social Cost, Journal of Law and Economics 3 (1960),1 (15 et seq.); Williamson, Transaction-cost Economics, Journal of Law and Economics 3 (1979), 233 et seq.

[39]Schuppert, Verwaltungswissenschaft, (Nomos, 2000), 575 et seq.

[40]Fundamental for the internal structure of organisation Mayntz, Soziologie der Organisation, (Rowohlt, 1963), 81, 85, 89; alternative to the internal administrative organisation through institutions there can also be an external administrative organisation carried out by the market, see Williamson, Transaction-cost Economics, Journal of Law and Economics 3 (1979), 233 (234 et seq).

[41]Williamson, The Economic Institutions of Capitalism – Firms, Markets, Relational Contracting, (Free Press, 1985), 15 et seq.; 68 et seq.; 402 et seq.; Arthur Benz, Einleitung: Governance – Modebegriff oder nützliches sozialwissenschaftliches Konzept?, in Benz, Arthur (Ed.) Governance – Regieren in komplexen Regelsystemen, 2nd ed. (VS Verlag für Sozialwissenschaften, 2012), 11 (15).

[42]Williamson, Transaction-cost Economics, Journal of Law and Economics 3 (1979), 233 (239, 248 et seq., 259); Erlei, Leschke and Sauerland, Neue Institutionenökonomik, 2nd ed. (Schäffer-Poeschel, 2007), 200.

[43]North, Institutions, institutional change and economic performance, (Cambridge University Press, 1991); 5, 8.

The meaning of the terms *institution* and *organisation*, from the New Institutional Economics point of view, can be linked to the administrative scientific definition. Organisations are groups of individuals, sharing a common interest and trying to achieve a common goal.[44] The organisation of the individuals is done by the appropriate configuration of institutions.[45] Institutions are formal and informal rules that are defined in legal rules or in other regulations. They can also be passed down orally.[46] Linked they form a normative system equipped with instruments that can purposefully control the behaviour of individuals.[47] Institutional arrangements can particularly regulate that certain bodies find out and transmit information and that certain bodies are bound by instructions. Furthermore, certain bodies have to be consulted about relevant organisational wise issues and be involved; they have the opportunity to comment and to participate.

Transferred to banking regulation, organisations are all national regulatory authorities and European regulatory actors pursuing the regulation of markets. To order and coordinate them, institutions are necessary. The economic concept of institutions means the legal bases (including laws, regulations and statutes) of the players in the financial market regulation and in the banking regulation. They form a set of operating rules that determines, among other things, who is responsible for decisions in a particular area and what procedures must be followed.[48] Institutions gained considerable importance in particular in terms of regulating information relations between different organisations.

### 2.3.3 Purpose of the Organisation

The constitutive legal basis of the organisation sets its legal form to the outside and structures the internal structure via its institutional arrangements. In addition, it sets special requirements or targets. They affect the organisational units both, from the inside and the outside: individual bodies can pursue internal aims; the organisation itself helps to purposefully fulfil the public service to the outside. The purposes of the organisation influence the administrative action. Having a set purpose,

---

[44]North, Institutions, institutional change and economic performance, (Cambridge University Press, 1991), 5, 74.

[45]Erlei, Leschke and Sauerland, Neue Institutionenökonomik, 2nd ed. (Schäffer-Poeschel, 2007), 22, 65; Richter and Furobotn, Neue Institutionenökonomik, 4th ed. (Mohr Siebeck, 2010), 7 et seq.

[46]Erlei, Leschke and Sauerland, Neue Institutionenökonomik, 2nd ed. (Schäffer-Poeschel, 2007), 22; Thieme, Verwaltungslehre, 4th ed. (Carl Heymanns, 1984), § 35 para. 211.

[47]North, Institutions, institutional change and economic performance, (Cambridge University Press, 1991), 3 et seq.; Leschke, Regulierungstheorie aus ökonomischer Sicht, in Fehling and Ruffert (Eds.), Regulierungsrecht, (Mohr Siebeck, 2010), § 6 para. 13; Thieme, Verwaltungslehre, 4th ed. (Carl Heymanns, 1984), § 35 para. 209; Groß, Das Kollegialprinzip in der Verwaltungsorganisation, (Mohr Siebeck, 1999), 13.

[48]Arrow, Essays in the theory of risk-bearing, (North-Holland, 1971), 224 et seq.

administrative decisions of individual organs and the whole organisation are directed in a particular direction. Purposes are defined by legal norms, government programmes and mere tradition; they can also be determined by administrative action.[49] They serve as orientation and scale for administrative actions.[50]

In context of the banking regulation, the financial market regulation sets purposes which are formulated very vaguely due to the large number of actors. They range from the development, to promotion and implementation of effective regulatory and supervisory policies. They also strengthen the rules and procedures at an international level through the consistent and effective implementation of regulatory measures at a supranational level. They too reduce damages in the credit system and losses of obligees at a national level. A common aspect of the institutional purposes is the contribution to the cooperation with other regulatory actors in order to protect the stability of the financial system.

### *2.3.4 Principles of the Organisation*

The internal design of formal structures of the organisation itself is relevant for the decision-making process.[51] It can follow different principles of organisation: in earlier times hierarchically-monocratic organisational principles prevailed. Hierarchical organisations and its bodies result in a single head from which the organisation breaks down at different levels. They are ordered from top to bottom and are controlled—along with rights and obligations, in particular the right to information and the obligation to report.[52] This allows to gain an overview over all processes very fast. Consequently, the coordination of the administrative organisation gets easier. In contrast, information and reports focus on a hierarchically privileged unit.[53] With that, the intellectual potential of the organisation or its bodies is weakened.

More recently, organisations were structured into chambers, departments or committees according to the collegial principle.[54] Thus, decisions are made by the interaction of several actors by majority. The collegial principle is preferred to the

[49]Thieme, Verwaltungslehre, 4th ed. (Carl Heymanns, 1984), § 35 para. 210.

[50]For a critical analysis see Mayntz, Soziologie der Organisation, (Rowohlt, 1963), 44, 136 especially when an organisation purposes several objectives without clear prioritisation.

[51]Trute, Methodik der Herstellung und Darstellung verwaltungsrechtlicher Entscheidungen, in Schmidt-Aßmann and Hoffmann-Riem (Eds.) Methoden der Verwaltungsrechtswissenschaft, (Nomos, 2004), 293 (307).

[52]Thieme, Verwaltungslehre, 4th ed. (Carl Heymanns, 1984), § 41 para. 243; Ellwein, Regieren und Verwalten, (Westdeutscher Verlag, 1976), 101 et seq.

[53]Luhmann, Funktionen und Folgen formaler Organisation, 2nd ed. (Duncker & Humblot, 1976), 198 et seq.

[54]Groß, Das Kollegialprinzip in der Verwaltungsorganisation, (Mohr Siebeck, 1999).

hierarchical forms as basic organisational principle.[55] This can be noticed on the basis of a two-staged decision-making process, which in turn connects the hierarchical with the collegial organisational principle. At first, the technical examinations take place at a horizontal level. This implies that size, responsibilities and procedures of the College are properly regulated.[56] Otherwise collegial organisations run the risk to destabilise or to get blocked in details. Through the cooperation of collegial equals, technical specialisations and practical experiences can be integrated in the decision-making process. Information paths are shorter in a College than in established hierarchies and the contributions of the Colleges can be coordinated horizontally. This results in a pluralistic decision-making, which in turn affects the understanding and trust in collegial forms of organisation.

Between the traditional organisational forms of hierarchy and the College there is also a less sharply drawn organisational principle. It can be described as Forum.[57] It is an organisational principle that emancipated itself from the hierarchical or collegial principle. It developed either from collegial relationships and organisational forms or distanced itself from a collegial organisational form with a strong hierarchical integration. A Forum breaks out from the prevailing relationships to organisational structures with hierarchical or collegial organisational principles. Outdated structures in connection with over-formalised methods caused this development. Forums are formed in areas of informal cooperation and usually have no superior and subordination relation. Organisations communicate and negotiate with each other in Forums. They cooperate when they have to carry out complex tasks where several parties with different information and resources work together. Then they divide responsibilities equally among each other.[58] Again, this is based on institutions defined as the sum of rules shaping the interaction. In addition, Forums are mostly informal groups that come together for advisory services but they do not act decisively.

Although the banking regulation needs to make concrete regulatory decisions, they also turn away from strictly hierarchical organisational principles and turn towards open Colleges or Forums. At a national level, decisions are still predominantly made hierarchically in departments or committees. At a supranational level, collegial structures have increased. However, the European Central Bank may give the impression that hierarchical decision-making prevails in recent fiscal and monetary policy measures. At an international level only Forums exist as principles

[55]Thieme, Verwaltungslehre, 4th ed. (Carl Heymanns, 1984), § 41 paras. 245 et seq.; Mayntz, Governance im modernen Staat, in Benz, Arthur (Ed.), Governance - Regieren in komplexen Regelsystemen, 2nd ed. (VS Verlag für Sozialwissenschaften, 2012), 65 (72).

[56]Thieme, Verwaltungslehre, 4th ed. (Carl Heymanns, 1984), § 42 para. 248.

[57]Thieme, Verwaltungslehre, 4th ed. (Carl Heymanns, 1984), § 42 para. 249 describes a similar form of the team principle. Further encourage to form this organisational principle originate from Luhmann, Funktionen und Folgen formaler Organisation, 2nd ed. (Duncker & Humblot, 1976), 324 et seq.

[58]Schuppert, Verwaltungswissenschaft, (Nomos, 2000), 596 et seq.; Trute, Die Verwaltung und das Verwaltungsrecht zwischen gesellschaftlicher Selbstregulierung und staatlicher Steuerung, Deutsches Verwaltungsblatt (1996), 950 (962 et seq.).

for regulatory decisions. There are two main reasons: Administration is already subject to actual uncertainties. Furthermore, especially in terms of regulation, great uncertainties rule over the economic development of markets and competition. There is a great need for knowledge and information, which is easier to satisfy by a discursive exchange during the decision-making process.

### *2.3.5 Tasks of the Organisation*

Administrative organisations meet specific tasks. General tasks range from programming, to execution and to controlling measures. Administrative organisations are decision makers; either hierarchically through a person or collegially through a committee. Institutional arrangements assign the competence to select among decision alternatives. Decisions to program, to execute and to control are at the core tasks of an administrative organisation.[59]

In banking regulation the central tasks of administrative organisations are not exercised uniformly. Programming decisions are taken over by international administrative organisations, with participation of the national central banks and supervisory authorities. Implementing decisions move themselves from a national to a supranational level into the hands of the European Central Bank. As a consequence of the crisis control decisions grow in importance at European level, since they provide for sanctions.

### *2.3.6 Competences of the Organisation*

The tasks of an administrative organisation are assigned to a relevant body that has the competence to fulfil the task.[60] By distributing and coordinating the tasks within the organisation, a system is created that determines who has which authority to act. In this framework, the responsible units perform the decision-making of the organisation according to its competences to the outside. The competences extend from decisions of principle to individual decisions and counselling.[61]

In banking regulation, the competences between the national, the international and European organisations are asymmetrically distributed. International organisations are solely responsible for counselling, even if their recommendations and guidelines have a great factual effect. Essentially, decisions of principle and individual decisions are carried out increasingly at European level through the European Central Bank and

[59]Ellwein, Einführung in die Regierungs- und Verwaltungslehre, (Kohlhammer, 1966), 95 et seq.; Thieme, Verwaltungslehre, 4th ed. (Carl Heymanns, 1984), § 72 para. 404.

[60]For general information see Ellwein, Einführung in die Regierungs- und Verwaltungslehre, (Kohlhammer, 1966), 101 et seq.

[61]Groß, Das Kollegialprinzip in der Verwaltungsorganisation, (Mohr Siebeck, 1999), 106 et seq.

the European Banking Authority in cooperation with the European Commission. In contrast, national organisations can only work on individual decisions that have no cross-border importance or on affairs without systematic relevance.

### *2.3.7 Organisational Relationships*

Organisational elements such as legal forms and institutions, duties and responsibilities, and particularly principles of the organisation relate to individual administrative organisation. Due to the continual convergence of life and business areas and its administrative units, administrative organisations can no longer be considered in isolation. Administrative units are interlinked through different information relationships and communication channels. Such compounds determine the influence of administrative organisations. In the following, "Organisational Relationships" are described as an essential element of the organisation, as they take account for the changed role of the administration.

Administrative organisations contact other administrative organisations. Communication structures are created that evolve.[62] Communication between administrative organisations often starts simultaneously. Structures built up in which the communication takes place. Subsequently a communicative exchange is created for one another. The development of these communication structures[63] takes place as follows: Some actors can initiate communication, while others can only receive communication. Hence, different communication paths are formed. These communication paths transport information. Information can be experiences or data (e.g., commercial practices or financial instruments of individual financial institutes, equity ratios, liquidity ratios). Information is essential for organisations to maintain and develop the administrative organisations. Furthermore, information is a requirement for rational decision-making.[64] Therefore, all administrative organisations have a special interest in a shared communication for obtaining information. Therewith, organisational relationships between administrative organisations are

---

[62]In general, this development is called Governance, Bang, Governance as political communication, in Bang (Ed.), Governance as social and political communication, (Manchester University Press, 2003), 7 (7, 9); Mayntz, New challenges to governance theory, in Bang (Ed.), Governance as social and political communication, (Manchester University Press, 2003), 27 (27, 35); Arthur Benz, Einleitung: Governance – Modebegriff oder nützliches sozialwissenschaftliches Konzept?, in Benz, Arthur (Ed.) Governance – Regieren in komplexen Regelsystemen, 2nd ed. (VS Verlag für Sozialwissenschaften, 2012), 11 (12 et seq.).

[63]Fundamental for basic understanding Luhmann, Funktionen und Folgen formaler Organisation, 2nd ed. (Duncker & Humblot, 1976), 190 et seq.; jurisprudential adopted by Masing, Transparente Verwaltung: Konturen eines Informationsverwaltungsrechts, 63 Veröffentlichungen der Vereinigung der deutschen Staatsrechtslehrer (2004), 377 (422 et seq.).

[64]Mayntz, Soziologie der Organisation, (Rowohlt, 1963), 96; Voßkuhle, Sachverständige Beratung des Staates, in Isensee and Kirchhof (Eds.), Handbuch des Staatsrechts – Vol.III, 3rd ed. (C.F. Müller 2005), § 43 para. 1.

created. Organisational relationships describe information relations.[65] Information relations are characterised by collecting and exchanging information. Further, institutional arrangements indirectly determine in which way information is processed to knowledge within the organisation. Information decides on the role of administrative organisation and serves the coordination of decisions in the European Composite Administration.[66]

Information relations are an important element of administrative organisations. This has two main reasons: national administrative units grow together within the framework of the European Composite Administration. In addition, the administration of economic sectors is getting more and more complex, meaning that an adequate administration of cross-border cases has an increased information and exchange requirement. Administrations learn and renew themselves, change their structures and adjust their relations to changes in their environment.[67] This development takes place in and through the administrative organisation, and is controlled by the Administrative Organisation Law.

In the context of organisational relationships, specialisations through divisions of labour occur. So, not every administrative organisation needs to collect, process and save every single information. Instead, they can concentrate on selecting, processing, transmitting and saving information.[68] Sometimes this may require a unilateral or bilateral cooperative exchange of information. Therewith, even in sectors with a large number of actors several loose and function-related communication and action relations are created.

These cooperative relationships are interdisciplinary operated under the name network.[69] It is a multi-level system of governments or administrations (e.g. central

---

[65]Siegel, Entscheidungsfindung im Verwaltungsverbund, (Mohr Siebeck, 2009), 56 et seq.

[66]Siegel, Entscheidungsfindung im Verwaltungsverbund, (Mohr Siebeck, 2009), 57, 260; Pitschas, Allgemeines Verwaltungsrecht als Teil der öffentlichen Informationsordnung, in Hoffmann-Riem, Schmidt-Aßmann and Schuppert (Eds.), Reform des Allgemeinen Verwaltungsrechts, (Nomos, 1993), 219 (261); basic information about administrative coordination in general and information networks in particular: Schmidt-Aßmann, Einleitung: Der Europäische Verwaltungsverbund und die Rolle des europäischen Verwaltungsrechts, in Schmidt-Aßmann and Schöndorf-Haubold (Eds.), Der Europäische Verwaltungsverbund, (Mohr Siebeck, 2005), 1 (5 et seq.;15 et seq.).

[67]Mayntz, Soziologie der Organisation, (Reinbek, 1963); 45 et seq.; Bang, Governance as political communication, in Bang (Ed.), Governance as social and political communication, (Manchester University Press, 2003), 12.

[68]For a critical view see Luhmann, Funktionen und Folgen formaler Organisation, 2nd ed. (Duncker & Humblot, 1976), 195 et seq.

[69]Schuppert, Verwaltungswissenschaft, (Nomos, 2000), 384; Schuppert, Verwaltungsorganisation und Verwaltungsorganisationsrecht als Steuerungsfaktoren, in Hoffmann-Riem, Schmidt-Aßmann and Voßkuhle (Eds.), Grundlagen des Verwaltungsrechts – Vol.1, 2nd ed. (C.H. Beck, 2012), § 16 paras 134 et seq.; Jansen and Schubert (Eds.), Netzwerke und Politikproduktion. Konzepte, Methoden, Perspektiven, (Schüren, 1995),10 et seq.; Möllers, Transnationale Behördenkooperation, 65 Zeitschrift für ausländisches öffentliches Recht und Völkerrecht (2005), 351 (364, 371); Möllers, Netzwerk als Kategorie des Organisationsrechts. Zur juristischen Beschreibung dezentraler Steuerung, in Oebbecke (Ed.), Nicht-normative Steuerung in dezentralen Systemen, (Franz Steiner Verlag, 2005), 285 et seq.

banks, financial authorities) of states. They are flexible, hybrid forms of organisation with a cross-border character.[70] Networks arise between a static, state hierarchy on the one hand, and a dynamic development of the market, on the other hand. Networks can do what hierarchies and markets cannot do. Through a cooperative work and information management, they ensure flexibility, reduce uncertainties by means of a mutual exchange of information and create knowledge through learning.[71] This points out the importance of organisational relationships.

This analysis sees organisational relationships as vertical and horizontal relationships between regulatory actors at a national and supranational level.[72] Vertical organisational relationships can be divided into unilateral and bilateral cooperative relations. Non-binding rights to consultation and statements are occasionally granted to perceive national interests and to maintain the work order of supranational actors. More common are binding duties of disclosure, which may range from exclusive obligations to provide information and duties to inform, up to durable obligations to create report and collect information. In contrast, horizontal organisational relationships show mutual forms of cooperation while programming an abstract decision framework or concrete decisions. Therewith, existing information is merged, empirical values are used efficiently and measures are coordinated.[73] In any case, Organisational Relationships are an essential element in areas that need much information and knowledge like the administration of regulation. Organisational relationships are particularly important for the regulation of the financial industry with a variety of different financial institutions.

[70]Groß, Die Verwaltungsorganisation als Teil organisierter Staatlichkeit, in Hoffmann-Riem, Schmidt-Aßmann and Voßkuhle (Eds.), Grundlagen des Verwaltungsrechts – Vol.1, 2nd ed. (C.H. Beck, 2012), § 13 para. 12; Schuppert, Verwaltungsorganisation und Verwaltungsorganisationsrecht als Steuerungsfaktoren, in Hoffmann-Riem, Schmidt-Aßmann and Voßkuhle (Eds.), Grundlagen des Verwaltungsrechts – Vol.1, 2nd ed. (C.H. Beck, 2012), § 16 para. 155.

[71]Eifert, Innovation in und durch Netzwerkorganisation: Relevanz, Regulierung und staatliche Einbindung, in Eifert and Hoffmann-Riem (Eds.), Innovation und rechtliche Regulierung, (Nomos, 2002), 88 (94); S. Augsberg, Europäisches Verwaltungsorganisationsrecht und Vollzugsformen, in Terhechte (Ed.), Verwaltungsrecht der EU, (Nomos, 2010), § 6 paras. 51 et seq.; Holznagel, Informationsbeziehungen in und zwischen Behörden, in Hoffmann-Riem, Schmidt-Aßmann and Voßkuhle (Eds.), Grundlagen des Verwaltungsrechts – Vol.2, 2nd ed. (C.H. Beck, 2012), § 24 para. 19; Jansen and Schubert (Eds.), Netzwerke und Politikproduktion. Konzepte, Methoden, Perspektiven, (Schüren, 1995), 12.

[72]For general information under the key word information relations in the European administration see, Schmidt-Aßmann, Verwaltungskooperation und Verwaltungskooperationsrecht in der Europäischen Gemeinschaft, Europarecht (1996), 270 et seq.

[73]Holznagel, Informationsbeziehungen in und zwischen Behörden, in Hoffmann-Riem, Schmidt-Aßmann and Voßkuhle (Eds.), Grundlagen des Verwaltungsrechts – Vol.2, 2nd ed. (C.H. Beck, 2012), § 24 paras. 37, 46, 48 b, 49.

### *2.3.8 A Summary of the Elements of Administrative Organisation*

Administrative organisations are characterised by different elements that are connected and influence each other. The comparison of certain elements in different organisations enables to systematically determine similarities and differences. It becomes apparent that elements of an administrative organisation interact. The synopses of individual organisations show systematic principles of administrative organisation. Those principles, in turn, help to classify individual organisations. In the following analysis, specific organisations are analysed in the field of banking regulation to create general models of administrative organisation out of particular phenomena.

## 2.4 The Concept of Regulation

The concept of regulation is a very young concept in the German and European science of administrative law. Its origin lies in the American Law of the 19th century. In the 20th century it was partly integrated or increasingly appreciated individually in the European Law. Meanwhile regulation stands in general for any state control of market activities in the public interest. Regulation can be characterised as an interdisciplinary cross-sectional task that involves the knowledge of economics and business administration.[74] An approach to the concept of regulation is based on wording and history, systematic and telos of banking regulation. On this basis, the functions of banking regulation are worked out (Sect. 2.5).

### *2.4.1 Regulation*

Regulation is a common term, both in science and in politico-media everyday life.[75] In addition to political science, economic and jurisprudence, also the daily news deal with reports on the regulation of financial markets. Is regulation merely a synonym for a trend or an instrument of economic management? In a context of a social momentum and differentiation regulation becomes particularly important for government and administration. Where does this term originate and what does it mean in general?

[74]Schmidt-Preuß, Das Regulierungsrecht als interdisziplinäre Disziplin – am Beispiel des Energierechts, in Baur, Sandrock, Scholtka and Shapiro (Eds.), Festschrift für Gunther Kühne, (Verlag Recht und Wirtschaft, 2010), 329 (331 et seq.) with numerous examples in the field of energy network regulation.

[75]Majone, The regulatory state and its legitimacy problem, 22 West European Politics (1999), 1; Ruffert, Begriff, in Fehling and Ruffert (Eds.), Regulierungsrecht, (Mohr Siebeck, 2010), § 7 para. 1.

A uniform definition of the word regulation does not exist.[76] The understanding of the term was traditionally based on the wording and grew in importance by transnational and interdisciplinary developments. It is noteworthy, that regulation is usually used in the context of interfaces of economic and legal systems.

As a result, regulation is a variable instrument, since it cannot be tied on a *single* model or a *single* goal, which explains why regulation is highly attractive for the state.

#### 2.4.1.1 Wording

The interpretation of the written wording in everyday language and in science is an approach on how to use the term. The English usage of "to regulate" and "regulation" is understood in a widely sense in legal, economic or technical matters. The Oxford Dictionary of English defines "to regulate" in the sense of "Control or maintain the rate or speed of a machine or process", "Set (a clock or other apparatus) according to an external standard", or "Control (something, especially a business activity) by means of rules and regulations".[77] In legal parlance, "to regulate" is defined as "rules and administrative codes issued by governmental agencies at all levels, municipal, county, state and federal. Although they are not laws, regulations have the force of law, since they are adopted under authority granted by statutes, and often include penalties for violations [...]" and "to control or direct according to rule, principle, or law."[78]

According to the wording, "regulation" means any state influence on business conditions and behaviour patterns of financial institutes on the financial market. In this work, "banking regulation" is understood both, in the sense of banking supervision and banking resolution. Banking supervision is interpreted differently in jurisprudence and economics. In a broader sense, the concept of banking supervision institutionally comprises all state bodies that are in charge of banking supervision.[79] In a narrower sense, supervision functionally means the compliance with all legal standards from the approval of the management to the termination of banking operations.[80] These opinions can be transferred to even younger and less discussed banking resolutions. As a result, in other reports the concept of banking regulation means all legal rules that control the formal organisation or the material execution of supervision and resolution for credit institutions.[81]

[76]Eifert, Regulierungsstrategien, in Hoffmann-Riem, Schmidt-Aßmann and Voßkuhle (Eds.), Grundlagen des Verwaltungsrechts – Vol.2, 2nd ed. (C.H. Beck, 2012), § 19 para. 1; Prosser, Law and the Regulators, (Oxford University Press, 1997), 4 et seq.

[77]Stevenson, Angus (Ed.), Oxford dictionary of English, 3rd ed. (Oxford University Press, 2010).

[78]Garner, Bryan A. (Ed.), Black's Law Dictionary, 8th ed. (Thomson West, 2004), 1286.

[79]Humm, Bankenaufsicht und Währungssicherung, (Duncker & Humblot, 1989), 35.

[80]Honold, Die Bankenaufsicht, (1956), 4 et seq.

[81]For a differing opinion see Wymeersch, The new European financial regulatory bodies, revue bancaire et financière (2012), 28 (29).

#### 2.4.1.2 Development of Banking Regulation

The law of banking regulation always developed in response to major financial crises or undesirable developments of individual financial institutions. In Germany banks were only liable to the *Gewerbeaufsicht* until 1931.[82] The Law of Banking Regulation developed as a special form of the *Gewerbeordnungsrecht.*[83] The world economic crisis of 1929 and the collapse of the Darmstädter und Nationalbank in 1931 led to the first legislative regulations by the German banking law of the German Reich,[84] which established a banking supervision. In response to the collapse of the Herstatt Bank in Cologne in 1974, the Basel Committee on Banking Supervision was established to coordinate banking supervision for cross-border institutions at an international level. In parallel, the international regulatory impulses were harmonised and implemented through directives and regulations within the European internal market. Increasing cross-border competition and the global digitisation of financial markets increased the business risk of the financial sector at the beginning of the 21st century. Through international banking, mergers of banks and the linking of the financial markets, crises are no longer restricted to individual credit institutes or markets.

Ensuring financial stability is an elementary responsibility of the state. Financial stability is geared towards protecting the financial market as a whole, transparency of the financial sector, as well as investors' confidence. To accomplish this task, the state is responsible for the regulation of banks and financial services providers. Initially, the state provides via central bank an infrastructure that co-founds, supervises, controls and intervenes in the financial markets.[85] In addition, the state ensures conditions for a competition in the public interest in the financial market.[86] In detail, this means that the state gives a normative framework. This framework is filled by financial institutions and is in turn supervised by the state and optionally enforced by the state.[87]

---

[82]German institution: state enforcement of laws and regulations regarding working conditions, health and safety at work; Bieg, Krämer and Waschbusch (Eds.), Bankenaufsicht in Theorie und Praxis, 3rd ed. (Frankfurt School Verlag, 2009), 60.

[83]German institution: laws regulating commercial and industrial business; Bieg, Krämer and Waschbusch (Eds.), Bankenaufsicht in Theorie und Praxis, 3rd ed. (Frankfurt School Verlag, 2009), 58, 62.

[84]Reichsgesetz über das Kreditwesen (KWG) of 05 December 1931 (RGBl I, S.1203), amended by the German Banking Act (KWG) on 10 July 1961 (BGBl I, S.881).

[85]Höfling, Gutachten zum 68. Deutschen Juristentag 2010, (C.H. Beck, 2010), F12.

[86]Höfling, Gutachten zum 68. Deutschen Juristentag 2010, (C.H. Beck, 2010), F9 et seq.

[87]Stober, Wirtschaftsaufsicht und Bankenaufsicht, in Pitschas (Ed.) Integrierte Finanzdienstleistungsaufsicht, Bankensystem und Bankenaufsicht vor den Herausforderungen der Europäischen Wirtschafts- und Währungsunion, (Duncker & Humblot, 2002), 21 (56), taken up and more differenciated by Junker, Gewährleistungsaufsicht über Wertpapierdienstleistungsunternehmen, (Duncker & Humblot, 2003), 41 et seq.

#### 2.4.1.3 Classification of Banking Regulation

In scientific papers, regulation is often equated with the regulation or the standardisation of a certain business matter. In particular, economics has a special influence on the determination of the regulatory concept. Regulation is in the public interest and serves to prevent exploitations and welfare losses. On the basis of this economically shaped term, the differentiation of the regulatory concept took place in jurisprudence.[88] Thus, legal statements in terms of regulation mostly relate to economic market issues. Regulation is regularly distinguished systematically between two dimensions: regulation in the narrower and in the broader sense.[89] Regulation in the narrower sense includes selected instruments of state economic law to create and safe competition on imperfect and non-existing markets.[90] Such markets are usually characterised by a particular structure. They are called networks. Networks are natural monopolies.[91] Through regulation, markets become contestable and prices are set. Regulation in the broader sense, however, describes any form of governmental influence on the economy and competition on the market.[92] Both, a legislative and an administrative intervention are possible. Common to both forms of regulation is that the state organises the competition by setting the necessary framework and guaranteeing a certain social level.[93] The area of banking regulation is a form of regulation in the broader sense. In particular, by statutory capital and liquidity requirements, organisational requirements as well as an administrative supervision and resolution, the State may both indirectly and directly influence the financial market and the financial sector.

---

[88]Berringer, Regulierung als Erscheinungsform der Wirtschaftsaufsicht, (C.H. Beck, 2004), 85 et seq.

[89]Schmidt-Preuß, Das Regulierungsrecht als interdisziplinäre Disziplin – am Beispiel des Energierechts, in Baur, Sandrock, Scholtka and Shapiro (Eds.), Festschrift für Gunther Kühne, (Verlag Recht und Wirtschaft, 2010), 329 (330) in addition to regulation in the narrower and in the broader sense he also distinguishes between regulation in a universal sense as any state interference in the market to achieve social goals (such as environmental or labor law).

[90]Eifert, Regulierungsstrategien, in Hoffmann-Riem, Schmidt-Aßmann and Voßkuhle (Eds.), Grundlagen des Verwaltungsrechts – Vol.1, 2nd ed. (C.H. Beck, 2012), § 19 para. 4; Masing, Grundstrukturen eines Regulierungsverwaltungsrechts, 36 Die Verwaltung (2003), 1 (5).

[91]Fritsch, Marktversagen und Wirtschaftspolitik, (Vahlen, 2014), 207; Knieps, Wettbewerbsökonomie. Regulierungstheorie, Industrieökonomie, Wettbewerbspolitik, 3rd ed. (Springer, 2008), 21 et seq.

[92]Proelss, Das Regulierungsermessen – eine Ausprägung des behördlichen Letztentscheidungsrechts?, 136 Archiv des öffentlichen Rechts (2011), 403 (405), points out that this understanding is mainly prevailing in the New Institutional Economics.

[93]Masing, Grundstrukturen eines Regulierungsverwaltungsrechts, 36 Die Verwaltung (2003), 1 (2 et seq.); Thiele, Finanzaufsicht, (Mohr Siebeck, 2014), 55 et seq.

#### 2.4.1.4 Sense and Purpose of Banking Regulation

Finally, sense and purpose of banking regulation are very important. Regulation is an instrument used by the Administration Organisation Law. It serves as a legal correction of market mechanisms in cases of market failure.[94] When a market fails, no competition takes place. Regulation in turn creates and promotes competition on the market. Basically, competition is a process of discovery.[95] Therefore, the Regulation Law cannot permanently stimulate a market but can only provide an arranging frame. Sense and purpose are basically determined by the circumstances of the objects of regulation and the resulting basic tasks. Banking regulation is a classic *Gewerbeaufsicht*.[96] The state monitors the risks of credit institutes to avert danger for other credit institutes, private investors[97,98] and depositors.[99]

Purposes of banking regulation are the protection of the financial services sector as a whole[100] and securing the market functions. The protection of the financial services sector as a whole focuses on the supervision of solvency and liquidity, to ensure the ability and the willingness to pay of banks.[101] In addition, regulation aims to repel systemic risk in the financial services sector.[102] Systemic risks are a danger for the business activities of banks, which are not confined to a single institution, but have negative repercussions on the overall economy through so called domino effects.[103] Banking regulation, therefore, focuses on so-called system-relevant banks, whose collapse cannot be compensated easily and could trigger other dangerous chain reactions.[104] By ensuring a workable, stable financial services sector with integrity also the confidence of bank customers of the financial

---

[94]Baldwin, Cave and Lodge (Eds.), Understanding Regulation, 2nd ed. (Oxford University Press, 2013), 9.

[95]von Hayek, Der Wettbewerb als Entdeckungsverfahren, (Institut für Weltwirtschaft, 1968).

[96]Röhl, Finanzmarktaufsicht, in Fehling and Ruffert (Eds.) Regulierungsrecht, (Mohr Siebeck, 2010), § 18 para. 82.

[97]An investor puts money into financial schemes, shares, property, or a commercial venture with the expectation of achieving a profit (see online, last downloaded 28.02.2015 at http://www.oxforddictionaries.com/definition/english/invest?q=investor#invest__23).

[98]Depositors are those ones among investors, of which the institution accepted money, not evidenced by documents, for repayment.

[99]R. Fischer in Boos/Fischer/Schulte-Mattler, KWG, 4th ed. (C.H. Beck, 2012), Einf. KWG, para. 120.

[100]Compare § 6 para 2 German Banking Act "counteract undesirable developments in the banking and financial services sector" referring to the purpose of Art 109 para 2 Basic Law for the Federal Republic of Germany "overall economic equilibrium".

[101]Röhl, Finanzmarktaufsicht, in Fehling and Ruffert (Eds.) Regulierungsrecht, (Mohr Siebeck, 2010), § 18 para.14.

[102]Gleeson, International Regulation of Banking, (Oxford University Press, 2010), 28 et seq.

[103]BVerfGE 124, 235 (246, 247) – Umlage für Bundesanstalt für Finanzdienstleistungsaufsicht.

[104]Ohler, Bankenaufsichtsrecht, in Ehlers, Fehling and Pünder (Eds.), Besonderes Verwaltungsrecht – Vol. 1 Öffentliches Wirtschaftsrecht, 3rd ed. (C.F. Müller, 2013), § 32 para. 18.

services system is protected.[105] The protection of market functions takes up on that. The protection of market functions is used to enforce standards of conduct for the business of credit institutions. Aim is to combat illicit financial operations and to protect the confidence of investors and depositors.[106] Therewith, investors as lender of capital are protected against taking high risks and against suffering high losses through the financial institutions as capital acquirers. The protection of the market function itself stabilises the financial services system as a whole.[107]

Sense and purpose of banking regulation focus on the key functions of business finances in terms of lending capital to companies and privates as well as in terms of influencing the economic policies via the central banks. States and central banks have not only a politically, but also a macroeconomical positive interest in ensuring the overall functionality of business finance to preserve jobs and to secure the financing of government task and to allow private pension schemes. In no other economic area the potential effects of a collapse of a single firm are so serious. This is because of the global interdependence and the special trust dependence of the whole system.[108] As a result, banking regulation promotes positive welfare effects and prevents negative welfare losses. Furthermore, the banking regulation creates a regulatory framework for the trust in transactions in financial markets and reduces information asymmetries between banks as providers and private persons as demanders.[109] Banking regulation is a versatile state instrument to influence the development of a major economic sector.

## 2.4.2 *Administration of Regulation*

Banking regulation is carried out by administrative units that are subjected to a differentiation, pluralisation and Europeanisation due to the development of financial markets.[110] In consequence of a growing interdependence between state and society, administration is no longer a monolithic entity, but a central control

---

[105] S. Augsberg, Rechtsetzung zwischen Staat und Gesellschaft, (Duncker & Humblot, 2003), 38 et seq.

[106] Röhl, Finanzmarktaufsicht, in Fehling and Ruffert (Eds.) Regulierungsrecht, (Mohr Siebeck, 2010), § 18 para. 15.

[107] Thiele, Finanzaufsicht, (Mohr Siebeck, 2014), 97 et seq.

[108] Thiele, Finanzaufsicht, (Mohr Siebeck, 2014), 91 et seq.

[109] Ohler, Internationale Regulierung im Bereich der Finanzmarktaufsicht, in Möllers, Voßkuhle and Walter (Eds.), Internationales Verwaltungsrecht, (Mohr Siebeck, 2007), 259 (260).

[110] Eifert, Regulierungsstrategien, in Hoffmann-Riem, Schmidt-Aßmann and Voßkuhle (Eds.), Grundlagen des Verwaltungsrechts – Vol.1, 2nd ed. (C.H. Beck, 2012), § 10 paras 17 et seq.; Schmidt-Aßmann, Verfassungsprinzipien für den Europäischen Verwaltungsverbund, in Hoffmann-Riem, Schmidt-Aßmann and Voßkuhle (Eds.), Grundlagen des Verwaltungsrechts – Vol.1, 2nd ed. (C.H. Beck, 2012), § 5 paras. 30 et seq.; Trute, Die demokratische Legitimation der Verwaltung, in Hoffmann-Riem, Schmidt-Aßmann and Voßkuhle (Eds.), Grundlagen des Verwaltungsrechts – Vol.1, 2nd ed. (C.H. Beck, 2012), § 6 paras. 60 et seq.

point.[111] Administration has opened itself for social influences. Administration also defines objectives in the best public interest for private actors.[112] In this interface, administration of regulation starts to work.

The concept of the administration of regulation shall not follow the widespread trend of the creation of neologisms in economic administration law which increasingly complicate a dogmatic order of administration. Rather, the administration of regulation clearly defines a specific activity of administration. Regulation can be classified into the dogmatic basic patterns of economic governance and economic management in the economic law. Economic governance is any state-initiated control action regarding compliance with a legal provision. Economic management is the controlled influence on economic processes.[113] It happens through target-oriented legal rules, whose implementation is monitored, appropriated and eventually corrected by the regulatory authorities.[114] Regulation is considered as a subcategory of economic governance, since its object is to meet regulatory requirements. Nevertheless individual instruments of regulation—such as capital requirements and liquidity ratios—affect economic operations of banks. Strictly speaking, regulation can be clearly assigned either to economic governance or to economic management according to its concrete form of appearance.[115]

## 2.5 Functions of Administration of Regulation

The development of banking regulation has shown that a market failure can be a reason for regulation. Hence, the central function of the administration of regulation is to order an economic sector. In the financial sector, the administration of regulation has several instruments: from authorisation to market participation, to the supervision of market behaviour, to an intervention in the market as well as to the

[111]Ritter, Das Recht als Steuerungsmedium im kooperativen Staat, in Grimm (Ed.), Wachsende Staatsaufgaben – sinkende Steuerungsfähigkeit des Rechts, (Nomos, 1990), 105; Trute, Verantwortungsteilung als Schlüsselbegriff eines sich verändernden Verhältnisses von öffentlichem und privatem Sektor, in Schuppert (Ed.), Jenseits von Privatisierung und „schlankem" Staat, (Nomos, 1999), 13 (15 et seq.).

[112]Trute, Die Verwaltung und das Verwaltungsrecht zwischen gesellschaftlicher Selbstregulierung und staatlicher Steuerung, Deutsches Verwaltungsblatt (1996), 950 (962 et seq.); Prosser, Law and the regulators, (Oxford University Press, 1997), 30, 304.

[113]Instead of many Huber, Öffentliches Wirtschaftsrecht, in Schoch (Ed.), Besonderes Verwaltungsrecht, 15th ed. (De Gruyter, 2013), Ch.3 paras. 176 et seq.; 187; 189.

[114]Kahl, Die Staatsaufsicht – Entstehung, Wandel und Neubestimmung unter besonderer Berücksichtigung der Aufsicht über Gemeinden, (Mohr Siebeck, 2000), 358.

[115]For different opinion see Ruthig and Storr (Eds.), Öffentliches Wirtschaftsrecht, 3rd ed. (C.F. Müller 2012), para. 23; Ruffert, Grundfragen der Wirtschaftsregulierung, in Ehlers, Fehling and Pünder (Eds.), Besonderes Verwaltungsrecht – Vol.1 Öffentliches Wirtschaftsrecht, 3rd ed. (C.F. Müller, 2012), § 21 paras. 24 et seq.; Ziekow, Öffentliches Wirtschaftsrecht, 3rd ed. (C.H. Beck, 2013), § 5 para. 6.

specification of market conditions.[116] Regulation affects the economic behaviour of market participants who are active or those who want to be active on a market. With different instruments, the administration of regulation can influence market participation or market behaviour. The regulation of market participation determines whether and to what extent a market player may be or should be active in a market[117] by assessing in particular the personal and professional suitability. Furthermore, the regulation of market behaviour regulates how a market player may or shall operate on the market[118] and determines what information must be passed on to the authorities. There is also the possibility to influence the market behaviour via concrete power to intervene. To use all instruments the administration of regulation in the European Composite Administration needs a multi-stage process to collect information, to generate knowledge and to execute.[119]

### *2.5.1 Regulation of the Market Access*

Credit institutes or financial service providers need government authorisation to be able to take action in the financial market business. Both the national and the European regulations contain a preventive ban with permit reservation. This means that banking transactions—on the understanding that special conditions are fulfilled—can only be allowed with an authorisation. This is to ensure that only personally and professionally suitable persons carry on a banking business or provide financial services.

The competence for the authorisation of business activities or for the withdrawal of the authorisation of systemically relevant banks, according to Art 6 (4) of Regulation (EU) No 1024/2013, is divided.[120] The decision to grant authorisation is a two-stage procedure: if the Member States comply with the authorisation requirements, the national supervisory authority proposes the authorisation to the European Central Bank (Art 14 (1)), which then gives a recommendation for a decision to the national authorities (Art 14 (2) of Regulation (EU) No 1024/

[116]Prosser, Law and the Regulator, (Oxford University Press, 1997), 5 et seq.; Bieg, Krämer and Waschbusch (Eds.), Bankenaufsicht in Theorie und Praxis, 3rd ed. (Frankfurt School Verlag, 2009), 64.

[117]Berringer, Regulierung als Erscheinungsform der Wirtschaftsaufsicht, (C.H. Beck, 2004), 95 et seq.

[118]Berringer, Regulierung als Erscheinungsform der Wirtschaftsaufsicht, (C.H. Beck, 2004), 94, 97.

[119]Fehling, Instrumente und Verfahren, in Fehling and Ruffert (Eds.), Regulierungsrecht, (Mohr Siebeck, 2010), § 20 para. 4.

[120]Schuster, The banking supervisory competences and powers of the ECB, Europäische Zeitschrift für Wirtschaftsrecht (2014), Supplement, 3 (4, 6 et seq); Gurlit, The ECB's relationship to EBA, Europäische Zeitschrift für Wirtschaftsrecht (2014), Supplement, 14 (14).

2013).[121] Finally, it comes to a national decision of authorisation by the national supervisory authority according to national law. However, the withdrawal of authorisation can be done at a European level for all Member States whose currency is the euro according to the European Central Bank via the Single Supervisory Mechanism Art 4 (1) lit. a) of Regulation (EU) No 1024/2013 in conjunction with Art 14 of Regulation (EU) No 1024/2013. The withdrawal of authorisation appears as a direct administrative act of the European Central Bank.[122] In fact, the European Central Bank, as a European Union institution, applies national German administrative law.

For all other banks, the authorisation to carry on a bank business or provide financial services is given by the German Federal Financial Supervisory Authority —but under supervision of the European Central Bank[123]—in accordance with Art 32 (1) German Banking Act (KWG). Any natural or legal person that provides professional financial services has an entitlement to the grant of an authorisation, if all necessary requirements are fulfilled and no ground for refusal exists.[124] Special requirements are placed to the personal reliability of the managing board and owner of the institute. However, the authorisation may be refused in case of the absence of professional competence.[125,126]

Systematically, this regulation structure corresponds to the principle of the German industrial law.[127] Withdrawal of authorisation is wholly or partially possible on the basis of Art 48 of the Administrative Procedure Act[128] if no specific legal basis is relevant.[129] Due to the reform of banking regulation in the field of

[121]In detail Art 73-84 of Regulation (EU) No 468/2014 of the European Central Bank of 16 April 2014 establishing the framework for cooperation within the Single Supervisory Mechanism between the European Central Bank and national competent authorities and with national designated authorities (ECB/2014/17), OJ L 141, 14.05.2014, p. 1.

[122]Neumann, The supervisory powers of national authorities and cooperation with the ECB – a new epoch of banking supervision, Europäische Zeitschrift für Wirtschaftsrecht (2014), Supplement, 9(12).

[123]Neumann, The supervisory powers of national authorities and cooperation with the ECB – a new epoch of banking supervision, Europäische Zeitschrift für Wirtschaftsrecht (2014), Supplement, 9(13).

[124]Requirements and grounds for refusal are regularly understood in a broad sense, leading to legal uncertainty for the credit institutes, Waigel, Deutsche Bankenaufsicht und internationale Bankenaufsicht, in Grieser and Heemann (Eds.), Bankenaufsichtsrecht, (Frankfurt School Verlag, 2010), 39 (44).

[125]§§ 33 para. 1 No.2 in conjunction with § 33 para. 2 KWG; § 33 para 1 No 3, 4, 4a KWG.

[126]Concretised through the Merkblatt der Bundesanstalt für Finanzdienstleistungsaufsicht and the Deutschen Bundesbank about the granting of authorisation to provide financial services according to Art 32 (1) KWG (online available as of September 2014, last downloaded 28.02.2015 at: http://www.bundesbank.de/Redaktion/DE/Downloads/Aufgaben/Bankenaufsicht/Informationen_Merkblaetter/merkblatt_ueber_die_erteilung_einer_erlaubnis_zum_erbringen_von_finanzdienstleistungen.pdf?__blob=publicationFile).

[127]R. Fischer in Boos/Fischer/Schulte-Mattler, KWG, 4th ed. (C.H. Beck, 2012), Einf. KWG, paras.133 et seq.

[128]Verwaltungsverfahrensgesetz (VwVfG) in the version of 23.01.2003 (Federal Law Gazette I, p. 102) as last revised on 25.07.2013 (Federal Law Gazette I, p. 2749).

[129]§ 35 (1) or (2) KWG: Expiry and revocation of authorisation.

banking supervision, the national regulations lose in significance as the economically relevant regulatory cases are mainly carried out at European level by the Single Supervisory Mechanism of the European Central Bank.

### 2.5.2 *Regulation of the Market Behaviour*

In the centre of banking regulation is the ongoing supervision. It ensures the stability of the financial system as a whole as well as the protection of investors of an individual institution.[130] Ongoing supervision is aimed at for the compliance of the authorisation conditions. All business operations of an institution are supervised, because not only risky business models, but also the accumulation of risks can lead to a threat to the existence of an institution and to threats to the financial system.[131] Systemically important banks are controlled in accordance to Art 9 et seq. of Regulation (EU) 1024/2013 of the European Central Bank. All other banks are subjected to the ongoing supervision of the Deutsche Bundesbank in accordance to Art 7 (1) German Banking Act. The objectives of the current supervision cannot be met solely by the supervisory authorities. Due to the richness and complexity of data, supervisors rely on the participation of credit institutions. Therefore, credit institutions are subjected to detailed duties to notify and reporting obligations.[132] Therewith, the respective supervisory authority gets all necessary information about the structure of the institute and its business operations as well as the professional and personal suitability of the managing board and the owner. The supervision gets a *disciplinary role*[133] due to the requirements to collect and process information. In addition to the extensive disclosure duties of banks to the regulatory authority, the regulatory authority has broad surveillance and monitoring powers.

A special occasion or a reasonable suspicion is not necessary. Both the European Central Bank and the Deutsche Bundesbank can make so-called special audits to perform their duties.[134] Here, the regulatory authorities may in part rely on private,[135] which makes sense given the whole host of institutions and the complexity of the matter, since it relieves personnel of the regulatory authorities. Overall, the

130 With further information Bieg, Krämer and Waschbusch (Eds.), Bankenaufsicht in Theorie und Praxis, 3rd ed. (Frankfurt School Verlag, 2009), 63.

131 Thiele, Finanzaufsicht, (Mohr Siebeck, 2014), 211.

132 In particular §§ 2a, 13, 13a, 14, 15, 24 et seq. KWG; Art 10 of Regulation (EU) No 1024/2013.

133 Thiele, Finanzaufsicht, (Mohr Siebeck, 2014), 212.

134 Via the German Federal Financial Supervisory Authority (BaFin) §§ 44 et seq. German Banking Act (KWG) or via the European Central Bank (ECB) Art 12 of Regulation (EU) No 1024/2013.

135 In Germany the account statement and the management report have to be examined by auditors § 340a in conjunction with §§ 264 et seq. German Commercial Code (HGB), They must present their results both to the Deutsche Bundesbank and the German Federal Financial Supervisory Authority.

ongoing supervision is a soft regulation of the market behaviour of credit institutions. As long as bodies subjected to the supervision work together with the regulatory authority, regulatory objectives can be achieved.

If ongoing supervisions come to the conclusion that financial institutions do not meet or do no longer meet the requirements for authorisation of business operations, banking regulation intend to use wide powers to intervene.[136]

The powers of intervention are mainly of an informal nature. They range from a request for a written opinion, a summoning to an interview, a binding test, and announcement of a legal opinion by the regulatory authority. Informal procedures are performed through discussions between regulatory authorities and the relevant financial institution. On the basis of the information requested, the supervisory authority communicates its position on individual operations and asks for the institutions statement. A communication process[137] between authority and institute appears. As a result, a large part of the differences is settled, which often leads to a change of the institutes praxis.[138] Otherwise, there is also the possibility of a check by the regulatory authority, which is usually very time consuming and costly for the institutes. It is also possible to announce the conception of legality through the regulatory authority. Even if such announcements are not related to a specific institute and have no direct binding force, they are actually very effective. Such informal interventions have an immense threatening effect.[139] In general, the financial institutes accept the recommendations of the regulatory authority instead of being presented publicly by a decision of the European Central Bank or an administrative act of the German Federal Financial Supervisory Authority. Such information is risky for the fragile confidence of the markets and can lead to a bank-run of the investor to the institute.

If the requirements for authorisation of the business operations are not or no longer met through informal interventions, the regulatory authority gets imperative powers to intervene for the protection of investors and depositors. Own resources entitlements are central, as well as liquidity requirements imposed on credit institutions by the German Federal Financial Supervisory Authority. The regulation of Art 10 (1) sentence 1, (1b) of the German Banking Act[140] determines that a financial institute needs to possess adequate own fund components to cover risks in

[136]Systematically, the system of the power to intervene is similar to the German police and regulatory law: a cascade of special (informal) powers to intervene has priority over a broad regulatory general clause and imperative powers to intervene.

[137]Fehling, Erscheinungsformen informellen Verwaltungshandelns, in Hoffmann-Riem, Schmidt-Aßmann and Voßkuhle (Eds.), Grundlagen des Verwaltungsrechts – Vol.2, 2nd ed. (C.H. Beck, 2012) § 38 paras. 13, 38.

[138]R. Fischer, in Boos/Fischer/Schulte-Mattler (Eds.), KWG, 4th ed. (C.H. Beck, 2012), Einf. KWG, para. 89.

[139]Thiele, Finanzaufsicht, (Mohr Siebeck, 2014), 217.

[140]Clearly defined on the basis of Art 10 (1) sentence 9 of German Banking Act through the regulation governing the capital adequacy of institutions, groups of institutions and financial holding groups of 06.12.2013, (Federal Law Gazette I, p. 4168).

the balance sheet. In addition to adequate own funds (solvability), Art 11 (1) sentence 1, (2) German Banking Act[141] requires a sufficient willingness to pay (liquidity). These requirements guarantee that obligations towards obligees are met adequately. They protect savers and depositors, who assume that they can efficiently dispose of their investments and remove them at any time.[142] In addition to the power of supervision, in future there are also differentiated powers of resolution through the implementation of the Banking Recovery and Resolution Directive 2014/59/EU in the Banking Recovery and Resolution Act. First, in its function as competent regulatory authority the Federal Agency for Financial Market Stabilisation can demand the drawing up of recovery and liquidation plans.[143] If a recovery is in danger a cascade of powers is opened, ranging from measures of early intervention, to the recall of the managing board to the provisional administration by the regulatory authority.[144] If there are resolution conditions,[145] shareholder and obliges can, in accordance to the directive, get a share,[146] and assets can be transferred to a third party or to a bridge bank.[147] The execution of the resolution tools is carried out through a resolution order.[148]

In addition, the national law for supervision contains a general clause in Art 6 (3) sentence 1 German Banking Act, which allows to intervene in cases of violation of regulatory provisions or in cases of undesirable developments. All supervisory standards, civil-law standards and criminal-law rules of the national and European law serve as model for the regulation of banking business.[149] Furthermore, a "grievance" can also exist without a violation of positive law when a credit institution differs considerably and in a persistent manner from standards and also is a danger for the object of protection of the banking supervision.[150] A precise definition of "grievance" has not yet emerged in literature and jurisprudence.[151] It is a

[141]Clearly defined on the basis of Art 11 (1) sentence 2 German Banking Act through Liquidity Regulation – Regulation on the liquidity of institutions of 14.12.2006 (Federal Law Gazette I, p. 3117).

[142]Ohler, Bankenaufsichtsrecht, in Ehlers, Fehling and Pünder (Eds.), Besonderes Verwaltungsrecht – Vol.1 Öffentliches Wirtschaftsrecht, 3rd ed. (C.F. Müller, 2013), § 32 para. 57.

[143]§§ 45, 45c, 46, 48a et seq. German Banking Act; §§ 12-21 Recovery and Resolution Act in conjunction with §§ 2-6 Credit Institution Resolution Act for recovery plans; §§ 40-48 Recovery and Resolution Act in conjunction with §§ 7- 23 Credit Institution Resolution Act for resolution plans.

[144]§§ 36-38 Recovery and Resolution Act.

[145]§§ 62 et seq. Recovery and Resolution Act.

[146]§§ 89 et seq. Recovery and Resolution Act.

[147]§§ 107 et seq. Recovery and Resolution Act.

[148]§§ 136, 139 Recovery and Resolution Act.

[149]Schäfer, in Boos/Fischer/Schulte-Mattler (Eds.), KWG, 4th ed. (C.H. Beck, 2012), § 6 paras. 36 et seq.

[150]Schäfer, in Boos/Fischer/Schulte-Mattler (Eds.), KWG, 4th ed. (C.H. Beck, 2012), § 6 para. 35.

[151]Ohler, Bankenaufsichtsrecht, in Ehlers, Fehling and Pünder (Eds.), Besonderes Verwaltungsrecht – Vol.1 Öffentliches Wirtschaftsrecht, 3rd ed. (C.F. Müller, 2013), § 32 para. 11.

vague legal term that shall be narrowly interpreted in the sense of constitutional certainty. Thus, a specific danger is necessary to either the safety of assets entrusted to institutes or to the proper implementation of the bank business and financial services.[152] Legal consequences can be orders within the meaning of Art 35 of Administrative Procedure Act.

The regulation of market behaviour through the intervention of the regulatory authority gives priority to the informal over the imperative instruments to avoid possible losses of confidence due to the public nature of the proceedings.[153] The regulation of market behaviour of banks is a special form of German *Gewerbeaufsicht* which follows the objects of police law of the protection against threats.[154]

### *2.5.3 Regulation of the Market Conditions*

The central regulation of market participation and market behaviour is supplemented by additional measures to regulate market conditions. These include internal in-house organisational and procedural mechanisms and general rules for the protection of the financial sector.

Organisational and procedural obligations serve for compliance and risk prevention.[155] Therewith, the possibility increases that credit institutes meet substantive requirements for market behaviour.[156] The organisational obligations include in particular a proper business organisation, as well as an adequate and effective risk management according to Art 25 a (1) sentence 1 and 3 of German Banking Act. Furthermore, credit institutions can ask for approval for in-house risk measurements at the German Federal Financial Supervisory Authority to meet capital requirements in accordance with Art 10 (1) of the German Banking Act.

In addition, regulations enable an action against financial crime[157] in terms of the fight against terrorism financing in accordance to Art 6a of the German Banking Act and for the anti-money laundering prevention under the Money Laundering

[152]Ohler, Bankenaufsichtsrecht, in Ehlers, Fehling and Pünder (Eds.), Besonderes Verwaltungsrecht – Vol.1 Öffentliches Wirtschaftsrecht, 3rd ed. (C.F. Müller, 2013), § 32 para. 12; for different opinions see Schäfer, in Boos/Fischer/Schulte-Mattler (Eds.), KWG, 4th ed. (C.H. Beck, 2012), § 6 para. 66.

[153]BVerwG, Decision of 06.11.2006, 6 B 82/06, Neue Juristische Wochenschrift Rechtsprechungsreport (2007), 492 paras 8 et seq.

[154]Ohler, Bankenaufsichtsrecht, in Ehlers, Fehling and Pünder (Eds.), Besonderes Verwaltungsrecht – Vol.1 Öffentliches Wirtschaftsrecht, 3rd ed. (C.F. Müller, 2013), § 32 para. 10.

[155]Röhl, Finanzmarktaufsicht, in Fehling and Ruffert (Eds.) Regulierungsrecht, (Mohr Siebeck, 2010), § 18 para. 63.

[156]Röhl, Finanzmarktaufsicht, in Fehling and Ruffert (Eds.) Regulierungsrecht, (Mohr Siebeck, 2010), § 18 para. 65.

[157]German rules refer to Directive 2005/60/EC of the European Parliament and of the Council of 26 October 2005 on the prevention of the use of the financial system for the purpose of money laundering and terrorist financing, OJ L 309, 25.11.2005, p. 15.

Act.[158] This allows protecting the business finance and consumers and preventing risks for the general public.[159] Bank regulation is a form of special-administrative law.[160]

## 2.6 Challenges of the Administration of Regulation

In times of a comprehensive globalisation and digitisation of financial markets through a high-frequency trade within seconds, the dynamics of the financial sector increased. Thereby, the economic and legal complexity of regulatory matters increased.[161] The performance of complex administrative tasks is complicated by inadequate legal requirements and rapidly changing market conditions.

The information needed by the state rises via the increasingly complex regulatory areas, while the resources for obtaining information decrease.[162] The state needs information in order to act rationally on markets, but the state cannot get this information by itself or only with the help of societal forces. Incorrect or poor information, lack of transparency or transaction costs lead to a lack of information.[163] Such a lack of information leads to uncertainties for the administration in the banking regulation. Banks deal with monetary expectations in the future.[164] An effective treatment of uncertainties requires knowledge.[165] Knowledge is a necessary precondition of each action in state and society.[166] It can be used both

[158]Gesetz über das Aufspüren von Gewinnen aus schweren Straftaten (GwG) in the version dated 13.08.2008 (Federal Law Gazette I, p. 1690) as last revised on 18.02.2013 (Federal Law Gazette I, p. 268).

[159]Ohler, Bankenaufsichtsrecht, in Ehlers, Fehling and Pünder (Eds.), Besonderes Verwaltungsrecht – Vol.1 Öffentliches Wirtschaftsrecht, 3rd ed. (C.F. Müller, 2013), § 32 para. 10.

[160]BVerfGE 41, 344 (355); BVerwG Decision of 24.06.1976, I C 56/74, Neue Juristische Wochenschrift (1977), 772 (773); Junker, Gewährleistungsaufsicht über Wertpapierdienstleistungsunternehmen, (Duncker & Humblot, 2003), 51 et seq.

[161]Benz and König, Privatisierung und staatliche Regulierung – eine Zwischenbilanz, in König and Benz (Eds.), Privatisierung und staatliche Regulierung, (Nomos, 1997), 606 (615, 632; 635); Wollenschläger, Wissensgenerierung im Verfahren, (Mohr Siebeck, 2009), 41 et seq.

[162]Willke, Supervision des Staates, (Suhrkamp, 1997), 10 et seq.; regards the States central function in gathering information and handling increasing uncertainties for the society; Herzmann, Konsultationen, (Mohr Siebeck, 2010), 35.

[163]Majone, The new European agencies: regulation by information, 4 Journal of European Public Policy 1997, 262 (266).

[164]Bumke, Kapitalmarktregulierung, 41 Die Verwaltung (2008), 227 (231).

[165]Knowledge is mainly understood as processed and systemised, see Scherzberg, Die öffentliche Verwaltung als informationelle Organisation, in Hoffmann-Riem and Schmidt-Aßmann (Eds), Verwaltungsrecht in der Informationsgesellschaft, (Nomos, 2000), 195 (200).

[166]P. Kirchhof, Mittel staatlichen Handelns, in Isensee and Kirchhof (Eds.), Handbuch des Staatsrechts – Vol.3, 3rd ed. (C.F. Müller 2005), § 99, considers knowledge as important as personal, financial resources and organisation for the administration.

retrospectively as explanation and foresighted as guidance to control[167] and avoid market failures with the help of regulatory measures.

The main task of banking regulation is to protect the stability of the financial system as a whole, as well as to protect investors and depositors through the regulation of market participation and market behaviour of banks in particular. Regulation is a dynamic task, which always takes place under uncertainties.[168] The regulatory authority does not know, among other things, the actual economic sums to guarantee solvency. Furthermore, the structures and risks of highly complex financial instruments and their partially immense leverage effect are only known to a limit. What is not known or is not recognised, cannot be subject to a legal control.[169] When one market side has more information than the other side, this is called asymmetric information.[170] Asymmetric information between regulatory actors and the regulated financial institutions is the central challenge of banking regulation.

### 2.6.1 Information as Resource of the Administration of Regulation

To ensure the stability of the financial system and to safeguard investors, the state misses important information. Information is based on data.[171] Regulatory administration firstly orders and interprets the available data in the factual context.[172] From this, information is obtained, which assigns a meaning to the data.[173]

[167]Schmidt-Aßmann, Die Ambivalenz des Wissens und die Ordnungsaufgaben des Rechts, in Röhl (Ed.), Wissen – Zur kognitiven Dimension des Rechts, Die Verwaltung Supplement 9 (2010), 39 (40 et seq.).

[168]Hirshleifer and Riley (Eds.), The analytics of uncertainty and information, (Cambridge University Press, 1992), 2 et seq.

[169]Appel, Methodik des Umgangs mit Ungewissheit, in Schmidt-Aßmann and Hoffmann-Riem (Eds.), Methoden der Verwaltungswissenschaft, (Nomos, 2004), 327 (328).

[170]Philips, The economics of imperfect information, (Cambridge University Press, 1988), 2 et seq.; Eichenberger, Wissen und Information in ökonomischer Perspektive, in Engel, Halfmann and Schulte (Eds.), Wissen – Nichtwissen – Unsicheres Wissen, (Nomos, 2002), 76 (79 et seq.).

[171]Albers, Umgang mit personenbezogenen Informationen und Daten, in Hoffmann-Riem, Schmidt-Aßmann and Voßkuhle (Eds.), Grundlagen des Verwaltungsrechts –Vol.2, 2nd ed. (C.H. Beck, 2012), § 22 paras. 7, 11.

[172]Albers, Umgang mit personenbezogenen Informationen und Daten, in Hoffmann-Riem, Schmidt-Aßmann and Voßkuhle (Eds.), Grundlagen des Verwaltungsrechts –Vol.2, 2nd ed. (C.H. Beck, 2012), § 22 para. 12; Trute, Wissen – Einleitende Bemerkungen, in Röhl (Eds.), Wissen zur kognitiven Dimension des Rechts, Die Verwaltung Supplement 9 (2000), 11 (14 et seq.).

[173]Albers, Umgang mit personenbezogenen Informationen und Daten, in Hoffmann-Riem, Schmidt-Aßmann and Voßkuhle (Eds.), Grundlagen des Verwaltungsrechts –Vol.2, 2nd ed. (C.H. Beck, 2012), § 22 para. 12; Schoch, Öffentlich-rechtliche Rahmenbedingungen einer Informationsordnung, 57 Veröffentlichungen der Vereinigung der deutschen Staatsrechtslehrer (1998), 158 (166 et seq.).

#### 2.6.1.1 Information Needed of the Administration of Regulation

Information is especially important for economically complex regulatory areas.[174] It is a fundamental basis for administrative decisions.[175] In particular, decisions regarding the regulation of banks do not exhaust themselves in the execution of acts. They require detailed information about the purpose and objectives of the measure, in order to not endanger or destroy the fragile confidence of the financial markets. Only by receiving information the regulatory authority can work; the processing of information enables the administration to adequately control its actions in the relevant factual context.[176] What information is gathered to what extent will affect the preparation and implementation as well as the content of decisions.[177] More information does not necessarily lead to better decisions. The state needs a high level of economic expertise to properly combine and process the information.[178] Then, information can reduce uncertainties about the reality and the administration has different choices for its decisions.[179] The regulatory administration initially encounters enormous lacks of information and is also faced with legal restrictions[180] in obtaining information with respect to the regulated financial institutes and financial intermediaries.[181]

---

[174]Majone, The new European agencies: regulation by information, 4 Journal of European Public Policy (1997), 262 (264).

[175]Schoch, Öffentlich-rechtliche Rahmenbedingungen einer Informationsordnung, 57 Veröffentlichungen der Vereinigung der deutschen Staatsrechtslehrer (1998), 158 (179); Siegel, Entscheidungsfindung im Verwaltungsverbund, (Mohr Siebeck, 2009), 55 et seq., 261.

[176]Holznagel, Informationsbeziehungen in und zwischen Behörden, in Hoffmann-Riem, Schmidt-Aßmann and Voßkuhle (Eds.), Grundlagen des Verwaltungsrechts –Vol.2, 2nd ed. (C.H. Beck, 2012), § 24, para. 1.

[177]Holznagel, Informationsbeziehungen in und zwischen Behörden, in Hoffmann-Riem, Schmidt-Aßmann and Voßkuhle (Eds.), Grundlagen des Verwaltungsrechts –Vol.2, 2nd ed. (C.H. Beck, 2012), § 24, para. 1.

[178]Spiecker gen. Döhmann, Staatliche Informationsgewinnung im Mehrebenensystem, in Oebbecke (Ed.), Nicht-normative Steuerung in dezentralen Systemen, (Franz Steiner Verlag, 2005), 253 (254 et seq.).

[179]Pitschas, Allgemeines Verwaltungsrecht als Teil der öffentlichen Informationsordnung, in Hoffmann-Riem, Schmidt-Aßmann and Schuppert (Eds.), Reform des Allgemeinen Verwaltungsrechts, (Nomos 1993), 219 (231); Hoffmann-Riem, Einleitende Problemskizze, in Hoffmann-Riem and Schmidt-Aßmann (Eds.), Verwaltungsrecht in der Informationsgesellschaft, (Nomos, 2000), 9 (13).

[180]Albers, Umgang mit personenbezogenen Informationen und Daten, in Hoffmann-Riem, Schmidt-Aßmann and Voßkuhle (Eds.), Grundlagen des Verwaltungsrechts –Vol.2, 2nd ed. (C.H. Beck, 2012), § 22; Holznagel, Informationsbeziehungen in und zwischen Behörden, in Hoffmann-Riem, Schmidt-Aßmann and Voßkuhle (Eds.), Grundlagen des Verwaltungsrechts –Vol.2, 2nd ed. (C.H. Beck, 2012), § 24 paras. 69 et seq., 74 et seq.; Fassbender, Wissen als Grundlage staatlichen Handelns, in Isensee and Kirchhof (Eds.), Handbuch des Staatsrechts – Vol. VI, 3rd ed. (C.F. Müller, 2006), § 76 paras 64 et seq., 77 et seq.

[181]Holznagel, Informationsbeziehungen in und zwischen Behörden, in Hoffmann-Riem, Schmidt-Aßmann and Voßkuhle (Eds.), Grundlagen des Verwaltungsrechts –Vol.2, 2nd ed. (C.H. Beck, 2012), § 24 paras. 1, 61 et seq.

#### 2.6.1.2 Information Deficit of the Administration of Regulation

A lack of information on the structure, business behaviour, capital adequacy or risk management complicates the regulation of banks. Economic expertise is necessary to overcome this lack of information[182] and an effective legal control to prevent regulatory authorities of standards dictated by the financial industry.[183] Since the state cannot merely expand or develop this business matter through trainings or recruitment of staff, obligations of banks to transmit information to the regulatory authorities as well as the powers of the regulatory authorities for examination increase.[184]

#### 2.6.1.3 Information Gathering of the Administration of Regulation

The information between regulatory actors and business finance is distributed asymmetrically. To gather information, regulatory authorities have to get involved in an exchange of information with private credit institutes or financial service providers at a national and supranational level.[185] The obligation to inform the authorities and the reporting obligation as well as auditing powers helps the regulator to gain extensive information that was previously known only to banks. Therewith, certain information asymmetries can be reduced or abolished.[186] If the information acquisition and processing is divided up among several actors at national and supranational level, the information is disseminated and available. A large number of actors can collect and process more information.[187] The communication between administrative units helps to collect, analyse, transmit and store information to use it in similar situations in the future.[188] If information is processed

---

[182] In parts of the administrative law an opening for descriptive related sciences aligned to social and societal changes is considered critical, see Lepsius, Steuerungsdiskussion, Systemtheorie und Parlamentarismuskritik, (Mohr Siebeck, 1999), 8, 30 et seq.; I. Augsberg, Selbstreferenz als Gesetzgebungsprogramm, Kritische Vierteljahresschrift für Gesetzgebung und Rechtswissenschaft (2007), 236 (253 et seq.); Wollenschläger, Wissensgenerierung im Verfahren, (Mohr Siebeck, 2009), 39.

[183] Majone, Regulation and its modes, in Majone (Ed.), Regulating Europe, (Routledge, 1996), 16.

[184] See above 2.5.2.

[185] Spiecker gen. Döhmann, Das Verwaltungsrecht zwischen klassischem dogmatischem Verständnis und steuerungswissenschaftlichem Anspruch, Deutsches Verwaltungsblatt (2007), 1074 (1077).

[186] Holznagel, Informationsbeziehungen in und zwischen Behörden, in Hoffmann-Riem, Schmidt-Aßmann and Voßkuhle (Eds.), Grundlagen des Verwaltungsrechts –Vol.2, 2nd ed. (C.H. Beck, 2012), § 24 para. 2.

[187] Spiecker gen. Döhmann, Staatliche Informationsgewinnung im Mehrebenensystem, in Oebbecke (Ed.), Nicht-normative Steuerung in dezentralen Systemen, (Franz Steiner Verlag, 2005), 253 (271).

[188] Holznagel, Informationsbeziehungen in und zwischen Behörden, in Hoffmann-Riem, Schmidt-Aßmann and Voßkuhle (Eds.), Grundlagen des Verwaltungsrechts –Vol.2, 2nd ed. (C.H. Beck, 2012), § 24 para. 4; Spiecker gen. Döhmann, Staatliche Informationsgewinnung im Mehrebenensystem, in Oebbecke (Ed.), Nicht-normative Steuerung in dezentralen Systemen, (Franz Steiner Verlag, 2005), 253 (272).

and organised into the already existing knowledge, deeper knowledge appears. Knowledge is an organised and systematic form of information.[189] Hence, knowledge enables an effective regulation of financial markets.

### 2.6.2 Uncertainties as Characteristics of Banking Regulation

The progress of the financial markets confronts the administration of regulation. For specialist administrations the uncertainties increase with a growing complexity subject-matters. In the area of banking supervision, the administration of regulation faces, for example, the challenge of imposing appropriate requirements on the provision of equity capital and of securing sufficient liquidity. Supervising the implementation of general ratios is again complicated by differences in different methods of calculation used for accounting in accordance with national or international accounting standards. Rather, the bank resolution meets immense uncertainties while determining resolution conditions taking into account other consequences. In these areas, law reaches the limits of its power to control; because what cannot be seen cannot be controlled.[190]

Regulation goes beyond the classical economic supervision, which monitors the economic activities of enterprises and selectively intervenes in case of maladministration.[191] The regulation of banks is an *active market assistance,*[192] figuratively speaking during the whole life—from birth to death. Regulation includes the life cycle of a bank—beginning with authorisation for taking up business, over the day-to-day supervision to the withdrawal of authorisation or the financial institute resolution. So, regulation ensures the functionality of a constantly changing economy field.[193] Active market assistance is not possible without sufficient information and knowledge. That outlines even more the importance of

---

[189]Hoffmann-Riem, Einleitende Problemskizze, in Hoffmann-Riem and Schmidt-Aßmann (Eds.), Verwaltungsrecht in der Informationsgesellschaft, (Nomos, 2000), 9 (12).

[190]Scherzberg, Wissen, Nichtwissen und Ungewissheit im Recht, in Engel, Halfmann and Schulte (Eds.), Wissen – Nichtwissen – Unsicheres Wissen, (Nomos, 2002), 114 (142 et seq.).

[191]Masing, Grundstrukturen eines Regulierungsverwaltungsrechts, 36 Die Verwaltung (2003), 1 (6 et seq.); Masing, Gutachten zum 64. Deutschen Juristentag, (C.H. Beck, 2006), D 48 et seq.; Herzmann, Konsultationen, (Mohr Siebeck, 2010), 39 et seq.

[192]Eifert, Regulierungsstrategien, in Hoffmann-Riem, Schmidt-Aßmann and Voßkuhle (Eds.), Grundlagen des Verwaltungsrechts – Vol.1, 2nd ed. (C.H. Beck, 2012), § 19 paras. 125, 127, with respect to banks if they are called market-optimising economic supervision, see Hecker, Marktoptimierende Wirtschaftsaufsicht, Öffentlich-rechtliche Probleme staatlicher Wirtschaftsintervention zur Steigerung der Funktionsfähigkeit des Marktes, (Mohr Siebeck, 2007).

[193]Ruffert, Regulierung im System des Verwaltungsrechts - Grundstrukturen des Privatisierungsfolgerechts der Post und Telekommunikation, 124 Archiv des öffentlichen Rechts (1999), 237 (246 et seq.); Schmidt-Aßmann, Perspektiven einer Systembildung, in Hoffmann-Riem and Schmidt-Aßmann (Eds.), Verwaltungsrecht in der Informationsgesellschaft, (Nomos, 2000), 405 (425 et seq.).

uncertainties in banking regulation. Once the uncertainty cannot be further reduced by information and knowledge, it gets highly relevant for the regulation authorities. The possibility and degree of the uncertainty must be considered individually for each decision.

### *2.6.3 Need for Knowledge and Knowledge Creation*

Increasingly, the administration of banking regulation needs to go beyond normative standards and needs to decide in an efficient, flexible and innovative manner. This leads to complex decision-making situations, especially when there are also uncertainties about the effects and action alternatives. In order to act rationally in such situations, the administration requires knowledge.[194] Knowledge is based on information. By processing, organising and connecting information with observations and experiences, knowledge is created and updated in a particular social context.[195] Thus, knowledge is a reliable criterion for actions.[196] In cases of regulatory uncertainties, banking regulation actors can choose the *correct*[197] measurement out of a set of action alternatives to solve a problem. This is necessary to be able to decide not only retrospectively, but also foresightedly on the market regulation of financial institutes. Knowledge is power especially in times when the sovereignty of the state over society decreases.

---

[194]Voßkuhle, Expertise und Verwaltung, in Trute, Groß, Röhl and Möllers (Eds.), Allgemeines Verwaltungsrecht – Zur Tragfähigkeit eines Konzepts, (Mohr Siebeck, 2008), 637 (641 et seq.).

[195]Trute, Wissen – Einleitende Bemerkungen, in Röhl (Ed.), Wissen zur kognitiven Dimension des Rechts, Die Verwaltung Supplement 9 (2010), 11 (16 et seq.); Röhl, Der rechtliche Kontext der Wissenserzeugung, in Röhl (Ed.), Wissen zur kognitiven Dimension des Rechts, Die Verwaltung Supplement 9 (2010), 65 (65 et seq.); Wollenschläger, Wissensgenerierung durch Verfahren, (Mohr Siebeck, 2009), 30.

[196]Scherzberg, Wissen, Nichtwissen und Ungewissheit im Recht, in Engel, Halfmann and Schulte (Eds.), Wissen – Nichtwissen – Unsicheres Wissen, (Nomos, 2002), 114 (119).

[197]Pitschas, Allgemeines Verwaltungsrecht als Teil der öffentlichen Informationsordnung, in Hoffmann-Riem, Schmidt-Aßmann and Schuppert (Eds.), Reform des allgemeinen Verwaltungsrechts, (Nomos, 1993), 219 (231 et seq.); correct is each comprehensible, rational reasoned decision, whose standards, forms and procedures result from the respective subject-specific law, see Voßkuhle, Sachverständige Beratung des Staates, in Isensee and Kirchhof (Eds.), Handbuch des Staatsrechts – Vol.III, 3rd ed (C.F. Müller, 2005), § 43 para. 1; nevertheless decisions remain rational imperfect, for a more differentiated opinion, see Voßkuhle, Expertise und Verwaltung, in Trute, Groß, Röhl and Möllers (Eds.), Allgemeines Verwaltungsrecht – zur Tragfähigkeit eines Konzepts, (Mohr Siebeck, 2008), 637 (640 et seq.).

The more the collected knowledge and experience by governmental regulatory actors decrease, the more the administration needs to fall back on private expertise.[198] Knowledge is in particular important for the administration of regulation. Knowledge and decisions are connected.[199] This becomes clear within the influence of organisations on decisions of the banking regulation.

The administration often makes decisions that affect the present or the future. Therefore, they need knowledge about current conditions and, in so far as this can be foreseen, conditions in the future.[200] This is also reflected in the administrative organisation. Government regulation actors meet the growing demand for knowledge through adapting and optimising the administrative apparatus to the new challenges. In particular, the recruitment of highly qualified professionals for the public service, the pooling of expertise in specialised organisational units and digital techniques become more and more relevant.[201]

Knowledge creation is the key to make decisions under uncertainties. The administration needs a special knowledge to meet the legal statutory principles.[202] Often, this knowledge is not available in the governmental organisation. As part of the European multi-level governance knowledge is produced in networks.[203] Through cooperation of regulatory actors, the respective regulatory knowledge can be used on many levels.[204] In this context, again the importance of administrative organisations and their influence on decisions comes out. Institutional arrangements of the administrative organisations initiate and control a process of collecting and processing information between the administration of regulation and the regulated financial sector.[205] Therewith, knowledge is obtained for concrete actions of the administration of regulation.

---

[198] Voßkuhle, Sachverständige Beratung des Staates, in Isensee and Kirchhof (Eds.), Handbuch des Staatsrechts – Vol.III, 3rd ed. (C.F. Müller, 2005), § 43 para. 53.

[199] Knight, Risk, Uncertainty and Profit, (Harper & Row, 1971), 197.

[200] Fassbender, Wissen als Grundlage staatlichen Handelns, in Isensee and Kirchhof (Eds.), Handbuch des Staatsrechts – Vol.VI, 3rd ed. (C.F. Müller, 2006), § 76 para. 37.

[201] Voßkuhle, Sachverständige Beratung des Staates, in Isensee and Kirchhof (Eds.), Handbuch des Staatsrechts – Vol.III, 3rd ed. (C.F. Müller, 2005), § 43 para. 2.

[202] Röhl, Ausgewählte Verwaltungsverfahren, in Hoffmann-Riem, Schmidt-Aßmann and Voßkuhle (Eds.), Grundlagen des Verwaltungsrechts – Vol.2, 2nd ed. (C.H.Beck, 2012), § 30 para. 28.

[203] Vesting, Die Bedeutung von Information und Kommunikation für die verwaltungsrechtliche Systembildung in Hoffmann-Riem, Schmidt-Aßmann and Voßkuhle (Eds.), Grundlagen des Verwaltungsrechts – Vol.2, 2nd ed. (C.H.Beck, 2012), § 20 para. 38.

[204] Wollenschläger, Wissensgenerierung durch Verfahren, (Mohr Siebeck, 2009), 34 et seq.

[205] Scherzberg, Wissen, Nichtwissen und Ungewissheit im Recht, in Engel, Halfmann and Schulte (Eds.), Wissen – Nichtwissen – Unsicheres Wissen, (Nomos, 2002), 114 (127); I. Appel, Methodik des Umgangs mit Ungewissheit, in Schmidt-Aßmann and Hoffmann-Riem (Eds.), Methoden der Verwaltungswissenschaft, (Nomos, 2004), 327 (354).

## 2.7 Conclusion on the Administrative Organisation of the Administration of Organisation

In times of a diversification and a pluralisation of the administrative organisation in the area of banking regulation, independent, collegial administrative organisations develop, which are capable of learning. Organisational structures as well as information and knowledge about financial markets become more important in order to find adequate solutions for increasingly complex economic issues.[206] Institutional arrangements help to define structures, tasks, competencies as well as the role of an organisation. The role of the organisation results from respective organisational relationships and information relations which are integrated in an organisation. It is a connected coordination structure between administrative organisations to gender and use information about financial markets and knowledge about the regulation within a supranational Composite Administration. Therewith, the organisation of banking regulation does not only determine the frameworks of the banking regulation, but also the business behaviour of banks and the functionality of the financial market.

[206] Vesting, Zwischen Gewährleistungsstaat und Minimalstaat, in Hoffmann-Riem and Schmidt-Aßmann (Eds.), Verwaltungsrecht in der Informationsgesellschaft, (Nomos, 2000), 101 (128).

# Chapter 3
# Models of the Administration of Banking Regulation

Banking regulation is a broad field that reaches from banking supervision, to regulation and implementation standards for bank businesses and to bank resolution. According to the variety of regulatory tasks, there are also numerous regulatory actors at a national, European and international level. In the following, actors of the banking regulation are classified and systemised with the help of characteristics of the administrative organisation. In this way, certain forms of actions and their context, as well as the influence of organisations on decisions can be deduced. They serve as paradigm to understand an economic regulation sector in the broader sense.

## 3.1 Parameters to Classify Model Types

A clear classification of the administrative organisation in the area of banking regulation is not possible. The classification is always subject to a latent valuation in the light of the political practice of banking regulation. Nevertheless, there are recurring elements of administrative organisations, which can be derived from the written and partially codified legal bases. They define the institutional arrangement, which in turn determines the legal form, organisation principles and tasks and competencies. Organisational relationships are already predestined, but they get their concretisation during the actual administrative practice. At the same time, each classification into model types will reach its limit, as the creation of models follows systematic considerations and no empiric analysis. The influence on decisions is programmed by the institutional arrangements, but the political and administrative practice of multi-level governance always leads to a shift of influence in the architecture of the administration of banking regulation. Moreover, the historical development of banking regulation can be used as basis for the systematic of the current banking regulation architecture, which in turn can be attributed to the figurative sense and purpose of banking regulation.



A. Wellerdt, *Organisation of Banking Regulation*, SpringerBriefs in Law,
DOI 10.1007/978-3-319-17638-3_3

### 3.1.1 Historical Development of a Banking Regulation System

Since the 20th century, the history of banking regulation has been mostly updated in response to the banking and financial crises. As a result of an economic and social interconnection of the world, activities of financial institutions have a globally greater influence. To establish a level playing field and to combat regulatory arbitrage, a European and international cooperation developed in the banking regulation.[1] In 1974, the current Basel Committee on Banking Supervision was established as standing committee under the name "Basel Committee on Banking Regulations and Supervisory Practices" by the President of the Central Bank at the Bank for International Settlement.[2] Herein, the Federal Republic of Germany is represented, beside the Deutsche Bundesbank, by the German Federal Financial Supervisory Authority.[3] The aim of the committee was to strengthen the stability of the international financial system. Members were ought to exchange information and experiences to recognise risks of a new international banking crisis at an early stage and to improve the respective systems of supervision.[4] Meanwhile, the Basel Committee on Banking Supervision has developed from a non-binding forum for the exchange of experience among banking supervisors with the help of votes of minimum standards to a widely recognised and binding authority that sets frameworks. Since 1999, the Group of Twenty (G20), as global agenda-setter and highest international legitimisation committee, supports the Basel Committee on Banking Supervision. The Group of Twenty is composed of the Heads of State and Government of 31 countries from both industrialised and developing countries[5] as well as the European Union. The European Union founded the Financial Stability Board (initially Financial Stability Forum) in response to the economic and financial crisis of 2009.[6] The Financial Stability Board is an informal dialogue forum; its membership includes representatives of national central banks and supervisory authorities, international financial

[1]Deutsche Bundesbank, International cooperation in banking regulation: past and present, 63 Monthly Report No. 9 (2011), 79.

[2]For the historic development: Basel Committee on Banking Supervision, A brief history of the Basel Committee, October 2014 (available online, last downloaded 28.02.2015 at http://www.bis.org/bcbs/history.pdf).

[3]Deutsche Bundesbank, International cooperation in banking regulation: past and present, 63 Monthly Report No. 9 (2011), 79 (80, 82).

[4]Deutsche Bundesbank, International cooperation in banking regulation: past and present, 63 Monthly Report No. 9 (2011), 79 (80).

[5]The members of the G20 are Argentina, Australia, Brazil, Canada, China, France, Germany, India, Indonesia, Italy, Japan, Republic of Korea, Mexico, Russia, Saudi Arabia, South Africa, Turkey, the United Kingdom, the United States and the European Union and extended by Algeria, Columbia, Egypt, Ethiopia, Haiti, Jamaica, Malawi, The Netherlands, Nigeria, Senegal, Spain and Vietnam.

[6]C.f. Thiele, Finanzaufsicht, (Mohr Siebeck, 2014), 534 et seq. for the development and role of G-20.

institutions and international regulatory and supervisory actors.[7] Aim of the forum is to generate an open and constructive discussion about the stability of the world economy and the functioning of global financial markets in order to decide over and implement an effective regulatory and financial market policy between developed and transition countries.[8]

The European Commission as member of the Financial Stability Board and as observer in the Basel Committee on Banking Supervision[9] combines the international and the European level. This has led to an organisational centralisation of actors of the financial market regulation in the European Union.[10] The European Union Member States have established a European System of Financial Supervision to secure stable financial markets. At the same time, the European System of Financial Supervision complements the independent European System of Central Banks—consisting of the European Central Bank and the national central banks of all Member States of the European Union—which are primarily committed to price stability according to Art 127 TFEU. The European System of Financial Supervision is an organisational construct not having legal personality.[11] It combines macroeconomic and microeconomic regulatory perspectives. For the micro-prudential supervision it can be helpful to have knowledge about macro-prudential potential dangers to identify institution-specific risks at an early stage. Conversely, information on certain risks associated with individual financial institutions is important to identify systemic risks for other financial institutions or the financial system.[12] Thus, a European Systemic Risk Board was established to enable a macro-prudential oversight of the stability of the financial system as a whole.[13] Risks are ought to be identified, banks shall be warned earlier and emergencies shall be avoided. In addition, three European Supervisory Authorities have been

[7]The member of the Financial Stability Board are countries and agencies (available online, last downloaded 28.02.2015 at http://www.financialstabilityboard.org/members/links.htm).

[8]Thiele, Finanzaufsicht, (Mohr Siebeck, 2014), 536 et seq.

[9]Ohler, Internationale Regulierung im Bereich der Finanzmarktaufsicht, in Möllers, Voßkuhle and Walter (Eds.), Internationales Verwaltungsrecht, (Mohr Siebeck, 2007), 259 (264).

[10]Communication from the Commission to the European Parliament and the Council, A Roadmap towards a Banking Union, COM (2012) 510, p.6 (online accessible, last downloaded 28.02.2015 at http://eur-lex.europa.eu/LexUriServ/LexUriServ.do?uri=COM:2012:0510:FIN:EN:PDF).

[11]Eriksson, Einheitlicher Europäischer Bankenaufsichtsmechanismus, Wissenschaftliche Dienste, 2013, 8 (online accessible, last downloaded 28.02.2015 at https://www.bundestag.de/blob/194116/1b35853890a67f88b660d07278354a9c/bankenaufsichtsmechanismus-data.pdf).

[12]Deutsche Bundesbank, European Single Supervisory Mechanism for banks – a first step on the road to a banking union, 65 Monthly Report (2013) No. 4, 13 (15 et seq.).

[13]Regulation (EU) No 1092/2010 of the European Parliament and of the Council of 24 November 2010 on European Union macro-prudential oversight of the financial system and establishing a European Systemic Risk Board, OJ L 331, 15.12.2010, p. 1; see in detail to this topic Deutsche Bundesbank, European Single Supervisory Mechanism for banks – a first step on the road to a banking union, 65 Monthly Report (2013) No. 4, 41 (43 et seq.).

established: for banks[14] (European Banking Authority), for market surveillance and security supervision[15] (European Securities and Markets Authority) and for the insurance business and company pension schemes[16] (European Insurance and Occupational Pensions Authority) to ensure a micro-prudential market supervision and a solvency supervision of financial institutions. In addition, at a macroeconomic level, the European Commission is represented as a voting member at the European Systemic Risk Board and, at a microeconomic level, as a non-voting representative at the European Banking Authority. National regulatory authorities are only involved in the micro-prudential oversight of the European Supervisory Authorities.

In Germany, the supervision is shared between the Deutsche Bundesbank and the Federal Financial Supervisory Authority (Bundesanstalt für Finanzdiesntleistungsaufsicht—BaFin). The Deutsche Bundesbank deals with the ongoing supervision of credit institutions, the Federal Financial Supervisory Authority takes sovereign supervisory and regulatory decisions regarding the credit institutes. The resolution of credit institutions, in turn, is done by the Federal Agency for Financial Market Stabilisation (Bundesanstalt für Finanzmarktstabilisierung). It is an institution directly under federal government control under public law within the portfolio of the Federal Ministry of Finance.

The history of financial and banking crises in the 1930s and 1970s, and especially at the beginning of the 21st century has formed a complex regulatory architecture at international, European and national level. Impulses at international level are usually addressed at the European level and legally solidified. Afterwards they are implemented in the interplay between European institutions and agencies with national authorities through supervisory, regulatory and resolution measures.

### *3.1.2 Sense and Purpose of Banking Regulation*

The historical development of banking regulation goes back to market failure events, resulting in a system of different organisations, which has developed on several levels that are based on the sense and purpose of economic regulation. Regulation is each sovereign exertion of influence on an economic sector which prohibits or commands a conduct within the meaning of regulatory objectives of a particular life or economic sector. The objective of banking regulation is to stabilise the financial system as a

---

[14]Regulation (EU) No 1093/2010 of the European Parliament and of the Council of 24 November 2010 establishing a European Supervisory Authority (European Banking Authority), OJ L 331, 15.12.2010, p. 12.

[15]Regulation (EU) No 1094/2010 of the European Parliament and of the Council of 24 November 2010 establishing a European Supervisory Authority (European Securities and Markets Authority), OJ L 331, 15.12.2010, p. 48.

[16]Regulation (EU) No 1095/2010 of the European Parliament and of the Council of 24 November 2010 establishing a European Supervisory Authority (European Insurance and Occupational Pensions Authority), OJ L 331, 15.12.2010, p. 84.

whole, by ensuring the functioning of the banking sector and protect investors from losses. In other words, banking regulation is based on the public interest in a functional and effective financial market in order to secure individual prosperity. Consequently, banking regulation—terminology it can be regarded as regulation in the broader sense—follows the overwhelming objective of any economic regulation: regulation avoids or takes up market failure events in multinational markets.

The Basel Committee on Banking Supervision, the Financial Stability Board and the G20 benefit from each other's regulatory impulses. Together they find an agreement on a global regulatory framework. The involvement of the European Union in the form of the European Commission helps to take up these impulses. Therewith, they do not fizzle out in the huge amounts of non-binding rules of international law of the 'soft laws'.[17] A coordinated legislation takes places at European level which is implemented with the help of European bodies and agencies in combination with the authorities of the Member States in the European Composite Administration. The jurisdiction and responsibility for the supervision of credit institutions remains basically at a national level, but increasing power shifts in favour of the European Central Bank with the Single Supervisory Mechanism, the Single Resolution Board and the European Banking Authority lead to a reversal of the system. It remains to be seen whether sense and purpose of the banking regulation are better achieved centrally at a European level rather than locally by the Member States. What seems pragmatically reasonable after the experience gained during the financial and banking crisis cannot yet be answered legally and economically—it remains to be seen.

## 3.2 Definition of Model Types of the Administrative Organisation

Modelling helps to classify and systematise various types of administrative organisations at an international, European and national level.[18] Parameters of the modelling are elements of administrative organisations which are shared by all types of organisation of banking regulation. Based on institutional arrangements, the legal form, the purpose of the organisation, the organisational principles, as well as responsibilities and competencies can be derived. In addition, organisational relationships are a special element of organisational types in multi-level governance due to the unilateral or bilateral information relations. From these elements, the study develops five types of models of the administrative organisation based on their respective influence on the decision.

The first organisational model of a regulatory actor as *developer* (Sect. 3.3) promotes the informational exchange between regulatory actors and serves the

[17]Giovanoli, Reflections on International Financial Standards as 'Soft Law', 37 Essays in International Financial and Economic Law (2002), 1(6 et seq.).

[18]This classification of model types is based on Wellerdt, Organisation der Regulierungsverwaltung, forthcoming.

generation of knowledge. Another organisational model can be viewed as *processor* (Sect. 3.4), who is incorporated by counselling and mediation in the regulation. Of particular importance is the organisational model of the *preparer* (Sect. 3.5), who determines decision-making programmes for either the regulation or rule enforcement for the national regulatory authorities at European level. The central organisation model in the field of banking regulation is the *implementer* (Sect. 3.6), who carries out regulatory decisions at a national level. The last organisational model is the *controller* (Sect. 3.7), who carries out the monitoring of the implementation of the regulation and the decisions of the regulatory framework at a national level.

## 3.3 Model Type 1: Developer

The organisational model of the developer is characterised by an informational exchange of experiences and information in order to gain knowledge for regulatory decisions and to provide impulses for a future regulatory framework.

### *3.3.1 Characteristics*

As the first organisational model of a regulatory actor, the developer is characterised by low institutional arrangements. Substantive legal bases range from political declarations or resolutions up to international treaties. They serve as an international platform for networking between public and private regulatory actors. The aim is to gather regulatory experience about the developments in the financial markets from different actors through an informal exchange of information and to build up regulatory knowledge. Such platforms follow no fixed principle of organisation, but bring together several parties without domination and subordination ratios. The central task of this organisational model is to promote the cooperation of several parties with different information and resources and to assume responsibility on a global level. In addition, this organisational model has no binding competencies, but the actors are able to take common positions in guidelines and formulate minimum standards for banking regulation. The organisational model of the developer is both directly and indirectly involved in the organisational relationship. Although not legally binding, guidelines and standards provide direct impulses for the regulation at the European level. Through the involvement of supranational organisations in these committees as member or observer, the results are also indirectly observed in the subsequent legislative process. Such international organisations develop material standards, which set standards for the regulation and implementation at European and national level.[19]

[19]Ohler, Internationale Regulierung im Bereich der Finanzmarktaufsicht, in Möllers, Voßkuhle and Walter (Eds.), Internationales Verwaltungsrecht, (Mohr Siebeck, 2007), 259.

## 3.3.2 *Form of Appearance*

In the area of banking regulation, the Financial Stability Board and the Basel Committee on Banking Supervision as well as Colleges of Supervisors for credit institutes can be assigned to the organisational model of the developer of regulatory standards and guidelines.

### 3.3.2.1 Financial Stability Board

The Financial Stability Board (FSB) is composed of representatives of national authorities and of one representative of the European Central Bank, the European Commission, the International Financial Institutions[20] and the most important Standard-Setting bodies.[21] The Federal Republic of Germany has a total of three seats and is represented by the Federal Ministry of Finance, the Deutsche Bundesbank and the Federal Financial Supervisory Authority.

Legal basis of the Financial Stability Board is a declaration of the Heads of Government and State of the G20 on the regulation of systemically important financial markets, institutes and instruments through the establishment of an organisation.[22] This declaration was confirmed by the Charter of the Financial Stability Board[23] within the international soft law. Sense and purpose of the Financial Stability Forum is according to Art 1 of the Charter of the Financial Stability Board the coordination of national financial authorities and international standard setters in order to develop and promote regulatory policies to ensure a global financial stability.[24] Consequently, the Financial Stability Board has developed from a pure coordinating body to an institution that acts as intermediary between nation-states and international standard setters. This decreases and partly eliminates existing deficits of legitimacy of the international standard-setting.[25]

[20]The International Financial Institutions are the Bank for International Settlements (BIS), the International Monetary Fund (IMF), the Organisation for Economic Co-operation and Development (OECD) and the World Bank, comp. Annex-A Financial Stability Board Charter.

[21]The international Standard-Setting, Regulatory, Supervisory and Central Bank Bodies are the Basel Committee on Banking Supervision (BCBS), the Committee on Payment and Settlement Systems (CPSS), the Committee on Global Financial System (CGFS), the International Accounting Standards Board (IASB), the International Association of Insurance Supervisors (IAIS) and the International Organisation of Securities Commissions (IOSCO).

[22]Declaration on Strenghtening the Financial System – London Summit, 2 April 2009 (online accessible, last downloaded 28.02.2015 at http://www.g20.utoronto.ca/summits/2009london.html).

[23]Charter of the Financial Stability Board, as amended and restated, was endorsed by the Heads of State and Government of the Group of Twenty, Los Cabos Summit on 19 June 2012 (online accessible, last downloaded 28.02.2015 at http://www.financialstabilityboard.org/publications/r_120809.pdf).

[24]Art 1 Charter of the Financial Stability Board.

[25]Thiele, Finanzaufsicht, (Mohr Siebeck, 2014), 543.

Organisationally, the Financial Stability Board is split into a Plenary, a Steering Committee and a Standing Committee.[26] These are supported by working groups, groups[27] and a secretariat.[28, 29] The Plenary is a consensual decision-making body, which adopts reports, principles, standards, recommendations and guidance.[30] The Steering Committee prepares the Plenary Meetings, establishes working groups and coordinates their work with the Standing Committees.

As part of its mandate, the main tasks of the Financial Stability Board include the identification of vulnerabilities affecting the global financial system, the monitoring of market developments, to promote coordination and information exchange among authorities responsible for financial stability and to support the establishment of supervisory colleges.[31] Furthermore, the Financial Stability Board cooperates with the International Monetary Fund to identify weaknesses in the international financial system and to submit appropriate proposals for reform.[32]

The members of the Financial Stability Board are obliged to adopt commonly agreed standards and to accept regular analyses of the financial markets by the International Monetary Fund and the World Bank.[33] In addition, the Financial Stability Board cannot create any legal rights or obligations for the national governments, their central banks and supervisory authorities or individual financial market participants.[34] In other words, the Financial Stability Board has no authority to legislate, implement or enforce. Their decisions are soft law.[35]

Nevertheless, especially the Key Attributes of Effective Resolution Regime for Financial Institutions[36] have an extremely far-reaching practical effect. They set

[26]Standing Committee on Assessment of Vulnerabilities, Standing Committee on Supervisory and Regulatory Cooperation, Standing Committee on Standards Implementation, Standing Committee on Budget and Resources, Art 14-17 Charter of the Financial Stability Board.

[27]Art 20 Charter of the Financial Stability Board.

[28]Art 22 Charter of the Financial Stability Board.

[29]Art 7 Charter of the Financial Stability Board.

[30]Art 9 (1), (2) and (3) lit. c) Charter of the Financial Stability Board.

[31]Art 2 (1) lit. a), b), c), f) Charter of the Financial Stability Board.

[32]Declaration on Strenghtening the Financial System – London Summit, 2 April 2009, para. International Cooperation codified in Art 2 (1) lit.h) Charter of the Financial Stability Board.

[33]Grande, Banking Regulation and supervision – developments and prospects at the global and EU levels, in Grieser and Heemann (Hrsg.), Bankenaufsichtsrecht, (Frankfurt School Verlag, 2010), 19 (31); Through the participation of non-national actors a certain neutrality is ensured during the preparation of reports and recommendations, c.f. Thiele, Finanzaufsicht (Mohr Siebeck, 2014), 544.

[34]Art 23 Charter of the Financial Stability Board.

[35]Ohler, Internationale Regulierung im Bereich der Finanzmarktaufsicht, in Möllers, Voßkuhle and Walter (Eds.), Internationales Verwaltungsrecht, (Mohr Siebeck, 2007), 259 (263); Giovanoli, Reflections on International Financial Standards as 'Soft Law', 37 Essays in International Financial and Economic Law (2002), 1 (25 et seq.).

[36]Financial Stability Board, Key Attributes of Effective Resolution Regimes for Financial Institutions, 2011, updated version published October 2014 (available online, last downloaded 28.02.2015 at: http://www.financialstabilityboard.org/wp-content/uploads/r_141015.pdf).

conditions and instruments for a (regular cross-border) resolution regime in order to enable a banking resolution without systemic shocks of the financial system and losses of taxpayers.[37] Furthermore, specific instruments are provided.[38] They form the legal basis for the regulation of banks at European level and are, if not in whole then in substance, adopted in directives and regulations.[39]

The inclusion of multipolar actors in the Financial Stability Board creates in fact numerous information relations, albeit without binding rights in the organisational relationship. However, the representation of numerous stakeholders allows a moral bond of the players to decisions and recommendations, which they have themselves worked out.

#### 3.3.2.2 Basel Committee on Banking Supervision

The Basel Committee on Banking Supervision (BCBS) at the Bank for International Settlements is composed of representatives of central banks and supervisory authorities from 27 countries.[40] The foundation of the Basel Committee on Banking Supervision was carried out on the basis of international law by a resolution of the Governors of the Group of Ten,[41] which can be attributed to the respective nation-states according to the will of the participating central banks.[42] However, the Basel Committee has no legal personality.[43] Purpose of the Basel Committee on Banking

[37]Preamble of Financial Stability Board Key Attributes of Effective Resolution Regimes for Financial Institutions.

[38]Chapter 3 of Financial Stability Board Key Attributes of Effective Resolution Regimes for Financial Institutions in particular transfer of assets and liabilities, establishment of bridge institutions, bail-in.

[39]Background is an understanding of the Group of Twenty to establish, in addition to the rules of the general insolvency law, a bank-specific resolution mechanism that allows a structured recovery, restructuring and, if necessary, a resolution, see Directive 2014/59/EC of the European Parliament and of the Council of 15 May 2014 establishing a framework for the recovery and resolution of credit institutions and investment firms, OJ L 173, 12.06.2014, p. 190; Regulation (EU) No 806/2014 of the European Parliament and of the Council of 15 July 2014 establishing uniform rules and a uniform procedure for the resolution of credit institutions and certain investment firms in the framework of a Single Resolution Mechanism and a Single Resolution Fund, OJ L 225, 30.07.2014, p. 1.

[40]Argentina, Australia, Belgium, Brazil, Canada, China, France, Germany, Hong Kong SAR, India, Indonesia, Italy, Japan, Korea, Luxembourg, Mexico, Netherlands, Russia, Saudia Arabia, Singapore, South Africa, Sweden, Switzerland, Turkey, United Kingdom, United States of America; observers on the Basel Committee are the European Commission, the European Banking Authority, the European Central Bank, the International Monetary Fund and the Financial Stability Institute.

[41]Belgium, Canada, France, Germany, Italy, Japan, Netherlands, Sweden, United Kingdom, United States of America since 1962 extended by Switzerland in 1983.

[42]Ohler, Internationale Regulierung im Bereich der Finanzmarktaufsicht, in Möllers, Voßkuhle and Walter (Eds.), Internationales Verwaltungsrecht, (Mohr Siebeck, 2007), 259 (261).

[43]Chapter 3 Basel Committee on Banking Supervision Charter.

Supervision is to strengthen the banking supervision worldwide and to enhance the financial stability by means of cooperation with a view to regulation, supervision and practices of banks.[44]

The Basel Committee on Banking Supervision only has a little internal organisational structure.[45] The Group of Governors and Heads of Supervision is the oversight body of the Basel Committee on Banking Supervision receiving reports of the Basel Committee on Banking Supervision and endorsement for major decisions. The Committee is the ultimate decision-making body[46] of the Basel Committee on Banking Supervision in which the heads of all authorities come together. Decisions are taken by consensus[47] among its members.[48] In addition, six working groups[49] and a secretariat[50] support the work of the Committee and prepare the meetings and drafts content.

Main activities of the Basel Committee on Banking Supervision are the exchange of information on developments in the banking sector and financial markets, the identification of current or emerging risks for the global financial system, the establishment and promotion of global standards for the regulation and the supervision of banks, as well as the monitoring of the implementation of Basel Committee on Banking Supervision standards in Member States and beyond with the purpose of ensuring their timely, consistent and effective implementation.[51] The major instrument of the Basel Committee on Banking Supervision is the setting of standards, elaborating guidelines and sound practices.[52] Particularly important are both, the preparation and publication of harmonised standards for the "International Convergence of Capital Measurement and Capital Standards" which became known under Basel I (1988), II (2004) and III (2010).[53] Describing it as international minimum standard idealises that it is a detailed full harmonisation of equity rights, which determines the implementation in the Member States.[54] The document "Basel III: A global regulatory framework for more resilient banks and banking systems" complements the Basel II document, which is further developed by new

---

[44]Chapter 1 Basel Committee on Banking Supervision Charter.

[45]Chapter 7 Basel Committee on Banking Supervision Charter.

[46]Chapter 8 Basel Committee on Banking Supervision Charter.

[47]Chapter 8.4 Basel Committee on Banking Supervision Charter.

[48]Ohler, Internationale Regulierung im Bereich der Finanzmarktaufsicht, in Möllers, Voßkuhle and Walter (Eds.), Internationales Verwaltungsrecht, (Mohr Siebeck, 2007), 259 (262).

[49]Chapter 9 Basel Committee on Banking Supervision Charter encompasses Accounting Experts Group, Supervision and Implementation Group, Policy Development Group, Macroprudential Supervision Group, Basel Consultative Group, Joint Forum.

[50]Chapter 11 Basel Committee on Banking Supervision Charter.

[51]Chapter 2 lit. a), b), c), e) and f) Basel Committee on Banking Supervision Charter.

[52]Chapter 12 – 14 Basel Committee on Banking Supervision Charter.

[53]For detailed information see Deutsche Bundesbank, International cooperation in banking regulation: past and present, 63 Monthly Report No. 9 (2011), 79 (80 et seq.).

[54]Ohler, Internationale Regulierung im Bereich der Finanzmarktaufsicht, in Möllers, Voßkuhle and Walter (Eds.), Internationales Verwaltungsrecht, (Mohr Siebeck, 2007), 259 (269).

regulatory requirements. Major changes concern the strengthening of the quality and quantity of equity, a global liquidity standard, the securisations of further risks with equity, measures to reduce cycles, debt ratios and a basic concept for the regulation of systemically important banks.[55] In particular, requirements for equity capital risk-related losses can be absorbed and the threat of bank insolvency can be reduced.[56] In general, the Basel standards serve the overall goals of banking regulation: the protection of investors, the stability of individual bank and the entire financial system. In addition, the Basel Committee on Banking Supervision published core principles for an effective banking supervision. These core principles set minimum standards for the supervision of systemically important banks, the identification of systemic risks, instruments for crisis management and for the recovery and resolution.[57] The Core Principles for Banking Supervision complement the Key Attributes of Effective Resolution Regime for Financial Institutions of the Financial Stability Board.

The decisions and recommendations of the Basel Committee are not legally binding, but rely on the commitment of its Member States.[58] Nevertheless, they are internationally recognised and implemented by the countries directly involved in the negotiations.[59] Thus, the Basel Committee gained high reputation as an international standard setter in the field of banking regulation. The standards are addressed to international banks and enjoy a high recognition, which often form the basis for supervisory practices in non-Member States.[60] Standards get additional self-assertion by being consulted by the International Monetary Fund as comparative rule for the assessment of national supervisory systems. The Basel Committee on Banking Supervision reports the results of its work not only to the Central Bank Governors and the Heads of the Supervisory Authorities of its Member States, but in consequence of the financial crisis also to the G20 Heads of State and Government.

Therewith, the information relations are enhanced and a greater involvement in the organisational relationships of banking regulation takes place.[61] As a result, the Basel Committee on Banking Supervision plays an influential role in the

[55]For detailed infomation see Bundesbankpublikation: Basel III – Leitfaden zu den neuen Eigenkapital und Liquiditätsregeln für Banken, (Deutsche Bundesbank, 2011).

[56]Ohler, Internationale Regulierung im Bereich der Finanzmarktaufsicht, in Möllers, Voßkuhle and Walter (Eds.), Internationales Verwaltungsrecht, (Mohr Siebeck, 2007), 259 (269).

[57]Basel Committee on Banking Supervision, Core Principles for Effective Banking Supervision, September 2012 (available online, last downloaded 28.02.2015 at http://www.bis.org/publ/bcbs230.pdf) paras. 19, 20, 24, 25, 39 et seq.

[58]Chapter 3 Basel Committee on Banking Supervision Charter.

[59]Deutsche Bundesbank, International cooperation in banking regulation: past and present, 63 Monthly Report No. 9 (2011), 79 (83).

[60]Deutsche Bundesbank, International cooperation in banking regulation: past and present, 63 Monthly Report No. 9 (2011), 79 (84).

[61]On the basis of Chapter 16 Basel Committee on Banking Supervision Charter.

international banking regulation, even though it has no legal personality and therewith no binding powers.[62]

#### 3.3.2.3 Colleges of Supervisors for Credit Institutions

To improve the cross-border supervisory practice, so called colleges of supervisors are established in order to coordinate the supervisory practice for banking groups operating cross-border that contribute to a group related convergence of the supervisory practices.[63] Legal basis for these colleges of supervisors are international treaties within the meaning of Art 131 of Directive 2014/59/EC.[64] A college of supervisors is a permanent structure for cooperation and coordination among the authorities responsible for and involved in the supervision of the different components of a cross-border group.[65] It is chaired by the entity's home supervisor. They are intergovernmental forums for the exchange of information between the supervisory authorities of the country in which the credit institution has its head office and the supervisory authorities of the countries in which the credit institution has a significant or systemically relevant branch. Aim is to coordinate and facilitate different supervisory practices in cross-border banking groups without decision-making powers.[66] Nevertheless, colleges of supervisors create comprehensive organisational relationships between the national supervisory authorities, whose information relations are defined within the framework of the European Banking Authority and the Single Supervisory Mechanism. This player makes an appearance rather as actor for the implementation of material rules for regulation and supervision than as formal organisation.

## 3.4 Model Type 2: Processor

The organisational model emerges through the counselling and mediation by the programming of regulatory frameworks and regulatory provisions. In particular, interests and impulses of different control levels are regularly processed and connected by national authorities and European institutions.

---

[62]Gleeson, International Regulation of Banking, 1st ed. (Oxford University Press, 2010), 33 (3.01); critical Ohler, Internationale Regulierung im Bereich der Finanzmarktaufsicht, in Möllers, Voßkuhle and Walter (Eds.), Internationales Verwaltungsrecht, (Mohr Siebeck, 2007), 259 (266 et seq.).

[63]Neumann, The supervisory powers of national authorities and cooperation with the ECB – a new epoch of banking supervision, Europäische Zeitschrift für Wirtschaftsrecht (2014), Supplement, 9 (13); Herdegen, Banking Supervision within the European Union, (De Gruyter, 2010) 2.

[64]Herdegen, Banking Supervision within the European Union, (De Gruyter, 2010) 41.

[65]Grande, Banking Regulation and supervision – developments and prospects at the global and EU level, in Grieser and Heemann (Eds.), Bankenaufsichtsrecht, (Frankfurt School Verlag, 2010), 19(33).

[66]Herdegen, Banking Supervision within the European Union, (De Gruyter, 2010) 56; Grande, Banking Regulation and supervision – developments and prospects at the global and EU levels, in Grieser and Heemann (Eds.), Bankenaufsichtsrecht, (Frankfurt School Verlag, 2010), 19 (34).

### 3.4.1 Characteristics

Another organisational model can be described as a processor. The European primary and secondary legislation mostly provide the legal basis, and establish collegial organisations, which are composed of representatives of the Member States, interest groups and bodies of the European Union. Central tasks lie in the recording of regulatory stimuli and processing them into concrete frameworks at a European level. Nevertheless, even this organisational model lacks essential own decision-making competencies for binding regulations. In fact, the competencies exhaust themselves in binding consultation-, participation-, proposal- and development rights in the enforcement of regulations and rules. They act as a mediator between the European legislative institutions and the Member States. Thus, it is in the nature of the assigned competencies that the processor serves as interface and agent in the organisational relationships between national and international level. This organisational model will play a key role in regulation between national interests and the European legislative process.

### 3.4.2 Form of Appearance

The European Commission and the European Banking Authority are the form of appearances as processor of international regulatory standards.

#### 3.4.2.1 European Banking Authority

The European Banking Authority is an independent agency of the European Union with legal personality[67] as well as a cooperation body[68] formed of representatives of the banking supervisory authorities in the Member States of the European Union as well as voluntary observers. The European Banking Authority has a double status as a European agency and as a member driven organisation. Legal basis for the establishment of the European Banking Authority is Regulation (EU) No 1093/2010 in the European System of Financial Supervisors. Aim of the European Banking Authority is to improve the quality and coherence of banking supervision in Europe, strengthen the supervision of cross-border groups and introduce a uniform European single rule book for financial institutions; all in cooperation with the national supervisory authorities.[69]

The European Banking Authority is organisationally composed as follows: the Board of Supervisors, the Management Board, a Chairperson, an Executive

[67]Rec. 14 of Regulation (EU) No 1093/2010; Art 5 (1) and (2) of Regulation (EU) No 1093/2010.
[68]Rec. 8 and 9 of Regulation (EU) No 1093/2010; Rec. 11 of Regulation (EU) No 1022/2013.
[69]Rec. 5 of Regulation (EU) No 1093/2010, Rec. 7 of Regulation (EU) No. 1022/2013.

Director and a Board of Appeal.[70] The supreme decision-making body is the Board of Supervisors. The Board of Supervisors is composed of the independent heads of all national public authorities, the non-voting Chairperson, and one non-voting representative of the Commission, the European Systemic Risk Board, the European Central Bank and the other European Supervisory Authorities.[71] In the Board of Supervisors, Germany is represented by the Federal Financial Supervisory Authority (voting) and the Deutsche Bundesbank (non-voting) as a body of ongoing monitoring. The Board of Supervisors shall give guidance to the work of the Authority and shall adopt opinions and recommendations.[72] Decisions of the Board of Supervisors shall be taken by a simple majority of its members whereas voting on legislations of a general nature such as regulatory and implementing standards as well as guidelines and recommendations require a qualified majority.[73] The Chairperson prepares the work of the Board of Supervisors for a term of office of 5 years.[74] The Board of Supervisors is supported and advised by the Management Board. The six members of the Management Board are elected from among the heads of the national authorities by the voting members of the Board of Supervisors.[75] The Management Board ensures that the Authority carries out its mission and performs the tasks assigned to it.[76] The Executive Director shall prepare the work of the Board and is responsible for the management of the European Banking Authority for a term of office of 5 years.[77] The Body of Appeal is composed of two representatives from each of the three European Supervisory Authorities; it is independent in making its decisions and is not bound by any instructions.[78] The decisions of the Body of Appeal may be appealed before the Court of Justice of the European Union.[79]

The main tasks of the European Banking Authority are the coordination between national supervisory authorities, which ensure the uniform application of the substantive financial market law and the supervision of the competent authorities in the

[70] Art 6 of Regulation (EU) No 1093/2010.

[71] Art 40 (1), 42 of Regulation (EU) No 1093/2010.

[72] Art 43 (1) und (2) of Regulation (EU) No 1093/2010.

[73] Art 44 (1) of Regulation (EU) No 1093/2010 in conjunction with Art 3 Decision adopting the Rules of Procedure of the European Banking Authority Board of Supervisors of 11 December 2013.

[74] Art 48 (1) and (3) of Regulation (EU) No 1093/2010.

[75] Art 45 (1) of Regulation (EU) No 1093/2010, the composition is determined by Art 8.4 Decision adopting the Rules of Procedure of the European Banking Authority Board of Supervisors of 11 December 2013, last recently the head of the European Banking Authority and the European Commission were represented by one non-voting participant Art 45 (2) of Regulation (EU) No 1093/2010.

[76] Art 47 (1) of Regulation (EU) No 1093/2010.

[77] Art 51 (1) und (3), Art 53 of Regulation (EU) No 1093/2010; Art 11.1 Decision adopting the Rules of Procedure of the European Banking Authority Board of Supervisors of 11 December 2013.

[78] Art 58 (1) and (2), Art 59 (1) of Regulation (EU) No 1093/2010.

[79] Art 60, 61 of Regulation (EU) No 1093/2010.

Member States. Specifically, the tasks include the development of technical standards, guidelines and recommendations,[80] the monitoring of compliance with the unional rules by national supervisory authorities,[81] the settlement of disagreements between competent authorities in cross-border situations,[82] the coordination of the created colleges of supervision within the sectoral legislation[83] and the monitoring of systematic risks emerging from cross-border financial groups.[84]

In particular, the supervisory Colleges of the European Banking Authority have important functions. First, a uniform application of the law shall be supported and a functioning of the colleges of supervisions shall be ensured both by the participation in colleges of supervisors.[85] Of particular importance is the ability to initiate and coordinate Union-wide stress tests for banks.[86] To guarantee the equivalence of supervisory rules and powers as well as sanctions in all Member States of the European Union, not only on the legislative level, but also in the implementation and enforcement, the European Banking Authority can design technical standards. By decision of the European Commission, these acts of law receive direct effect in the Member States. There are two different types of standards that are prepared by the European Banking Authority and adopted in consultation with the European Commission, the European Parliament and the Council. The regulatory technical standards[87] developed by the European Banking Authority and submitted to the European Commission according to Art 290 TFEU for approval.[88] The Commission may amend the content of the draft only in very limited cases, after consultation with the European Banking Authority. The adoption of a draft by the European Commission is followed by the forwarding of this draft to the European Parliament and the Council, which must raise their objections within a month.[89] Besides implementing technical standards[90] are developed by the European Banking Authority, which can be altered widely by the European Commission according to Art 291 TFEU, while the involvement of the European Parliament and the Council is limited to mere information rights.[91] Standards are published as Decision or Regulation in the Official Journal of the European Union. Guidelines

[80] Art 8 (1) lit. a), Art 10-16 of Regulation (EU) No. 1093/2010.

[81] Art 8 (1) lit. e), f), g) and Art 17 of Regulation (EU) No. 1093/2010.

[82] Art 19 of Regulation (EU) No. 1093/2010.

[83] Art 8 (1) lit. i), Art 21 of Regulation (EU) No. 1093/2010.

[84] Art 22-27 of Regulation (EU) No 1093/2010.

[85] Rec. 36 of Regulation (EU) No 1093/2010.

[86] Art 21 (1) lit. a), Art 32 of Regulation (EU) No 1093/2010.

[87] Matters subject to technical standards should be genuinely technical, to explain, develop or supplement the provisions in the basic acts, Rec. 12 of Directive 2010/78/EU.

[88] Art 10 (1) subparas. 1 and 2 of Regulation (EU) No 1093/2010.

[89] Art 10 (3) of Regulation (EU) No 1093/2010.

[90] Implementing technical standards shall determine a uniform application of binding acts of law and contain no political decisions Rec. 12 Directive 2010/78/EU.

[91] Art 15 (1) subpara. 5; (3) subpara. 3 of Regulation (EU) No 1093/2010.

and recommendations are not legally binding. However, the national authorities have to apply Decisions or Regulations or justify their non-application against the European Banking Authority, which in turn publishes the non-application.[92] Through these comply-or-explain mechanisms, the application pressure for the Member States shall be increased. In addition, the European Banking Authority can take over the settlement of disagreements between national supervisory authorities under the supervision of banks acting at European level and support or replace national authorities in the decision-making process in a crisis.[93] Specifically, the European Banking Authority can address binding decisions to nation supervisory authorities (direction) or to individual market participants (intervention). However, it has no powers to compel the enforcement of these decisions. The enforcement is in the responsibility of national supervisors.

The European Banking Authority is involved in a variety of organisational relationships through information relations to national supervisory authorities, via Colleges of Supervisors, the Commission in the standard setting procedure and to the members of the Board of Supervisors. This ensures the exchange of information and the coordination of supervisory practices through a coherent application of law across the Member States of the European Union.

#### 3.4.2.2 European Commission

The European Commission is in accordance with Art 13 Treaty on European Union (TEU)[94] a body of the European Union. It is composed of a representative of one of each 28 Member States. These so-called commissioners are nominated by the governments of the Member States and are confirmed by the European Parliament. They are authorised to commit for the Member States they represent and exercise the voting right. Legal basis of the European Commission is Art 17 TEU. Organisationally, the European Commission is headed by a president, who is assisted by six Vice-Presidents, who in turn control and coordinate 20 commissioners and their Directorates-General. The European Commission acts as a College that decides by oral advice or written by circulation under Art 250 TFEU with a majority of its members. The central task of the European Commission is preparing and introducing legislative initiatives with the help of the sub-structure of the Directorates-General and services. Rather, the European Commission is the representative of the European Union to the outside and carries out the role of the executive in the model of separation of powers in Europe. In the ordinary legislative procedure after Art 289 TFEU the European Commission plays an initiating role, as the legislative procedure is periodically initiated by a proposal of the Commission according to Art 294 (2) TFEU. By the drafting of legislative proposals

---

[92]Art 16 (3) of Regulation (EU) No 1093/2010.

[93]Art 8 (2) lit. e), (f); Art 17 (6), Art 18 (3) and (4), Art 19 (3) and (4) of Regulation (EU) No 1093/2010.

[94]Consolidated version of the Treaty on European Union, OJ C 326, 26.10.2012, p. 13.

in the Directorates-General and services, the European Commission can already influence the programming of acts of law. Through the cooperation of the European Commission with the Directorates-General and services a variety of information relations that have a huge impact on the decisions of the Commission in the organisational relationship.

## 3.5 Model Type 3: Preparer

The organisational model of the *preparer* has great influence on the settlement of decision programmes. Regulatory decisions are programmed either by specifying a European regulatory framework which requires the implementation of Member States or by a far-reaching and binding regulation in the Member States.

### 3.5.1 Characteristics

The organisational model of the *preparer* is of particular importance. Within the meaning of the administrative system in the European Union, the implementation of the law is usually done through an indirect enforcement in the Member States. The implementation of the law is based on decision programmes, which in turn are determined at European level. Preparers of regulatory frameworks and regulations in individual cases are bodies of the European Union, which are determined by the European treaties. Consequently, they pursue values and objectives of the European Union within the meaning of Art 2 and 3 TEU. The respective players consist of collegial (steering) committees that are proportionally represented by the Member States in accordance with the principle of representative democracy. Art 3, 4 and 5 TFEU determine the competencies of this organisational model, whose extensive tasks depend on the player and reach from proposal rights to participation and opinion rights to decision-making powers. In addition to formal organisational relationships between actors, this organisational model comprises also material information relations through the participation of authorities and interest groups in the Member States. Through the European legislative process, decision programmes are set in advance for the regulation or rule enforcement for the national regulatory authorities. Thus, the organisational model of the preparer gains decisive influence on decisions.

### 3.5.2 Form of Appearance

The preparation of regulation programmes for the enforcement by the respective authority takes place within the ordinary legislative procedure of the interplay between the European Parliament and Council as well as during the delegated legislation by the European Commission.

#### 3.5.2.1 European Parliament and Council

The European Parliament and the Council are, in accordance with Art 13 TEU, institutions of the European Union. The European Parliament consists of 750 directly legitimised representatives of Union citizens of the Member States. The Council consists of one representative of each Member State of the ministerial level, who may commit the government of the Member State in question and cast its vote. The European Parliament is a collegial body, which shall act by a majority of the votes, Art 231 TFEU. The Council is a collegial body whose decisions can generally be taken by qualified majority, Art 16 (2) TEU, Art 238 (2) and (3) TFEU. The European Parliament acts, jointly with the Council, in a legislative capacity and exercises the rights of action together with the Council in accordance with Art 14 (1), 16 (1) TEU.

In the ordinary legislative procedure, the European Parliament and the Council act equally together with the participation of national parliaments.[95] Proposals of the Commission are forwarded to the European Parliament and Council and also, if required by contract, to the European Economic and Social Committee and the Committee of the Regions.[96] A first reading in the European Parliament follows. The Parliament declares by a simple majority whether it approves or rejects the proposal or if it proposes any changes.[97] At the same time negotiations take place in the Council Working Groups, which closely include the national administrations in order to find a compromise of the Member States. The Council acts by a qualified majority, whether it approves the European Parliament's position[98] or adopts its own position,[99] which is to be fully communicated to the European Parliament. There may be a second reading in the European Parliament, which points out the opinion of the European Commission that claims which quorum applies for the second reading in the Council.[100] Often a so-called informal trialogue takes place in the form of informal meetings of representatives of the Commission, the European Parliament and the Council to come to an agreement outside the regular and avoid the invocation of an appeal of a conciliation committee by the President of the Council.[101] The legislative procedure comes to an end after finding an agreement with a formal decision and a publication in the Official Journal of the European Union. In this differentiated and complex procedure, guidelines and regulations for the regulation of financial markets and credit institutions are adopted. Directives give Member States a framework when implementing the Directive in national law, while the increased creation of regulations directly and immediately programme the

[95] Art 289 (1) TFEU, Art 12 (a) TEU.

[96] Art 294 (2) TFEU.

[97] Art 294 (3) TFEU.

[98] Art 294 (4) TFEU.

[99] Art 294 (5) and (6) TFEU.

[100] Art 294 (7) lit. a), b), c) and (8) lit. a) or b) TFEU.

[101] Haratsch, Koenig and Pechstein (Eds.), Europarecht, 9th ed. (Mohr Siebeck, 2014), 146 para. 327.

application. In this respect, the European Parliament and the Council have, with the participation of the Commission, a major influence on the establishment of consistent regulatory programmes at European and national level.

#### 3.5.2.2 European Commission

To discharge the European Parliament and the Council as legislative bodies, as well as to simplify and accelerate the alignment of legal acts to current developments, the legislative powers may be delegated to the European Commission as an exception to the legislative procedure.[102] In addition, executive powers over the Member States can be transferred to the European Commission.[103] In acts of law, which have been adopted in a legislative procedure, the competence to adopt non-legislative acts of general application to supplement or amend non-essential elements of the respective legislative procedure can be transferred to the European Commission according to Art 290 (1) and (3) TFEU. So-called delegated acts are only effective if no objection has been expressed by the European Parliament or the Council within a period set by the legislative act, Art 290 (2) TFEU. Regulatory technical standards of the European Banking Authority can be adopted as delegated act by the European Commission on the basis of Art 10 (1) in conjunction with Art 1 (2) of Regulation (EU) 1093/2010, especially in the context of the objectives and contents of Directive 2013/36/EU on access to the activity of credit institutions and the prudential supervision of credit institutions and investment firms. Therewith, regulatory technical standards specify approaches and methods of capital and risk assessment.[104]

According to Art 291 (1) TFEU Union law is generally carried out by the Member States. Exceptionally, the European Commission may adopt so-called implementing acts, if the Commission has been expressly authorised to do so and a union-wide uniform implementation is required, Art 291 (1) and (4). The adoption of implementing acts is done with the participation of committees of officers of the Member States. The implementing technical standards of the European Banking Authority can be adopted as implementing acts by the European Commission on the basis of Art 15 (1) in conjunction with Article 1 (2) of Regulation (EU) 1093/2010, especially in the context of the objectives and contents of Directive 2013/36/EU on access to the activity of credit institutions and the prudential supervision of credit institutions and investment firms adopt. Technical standards can also regulate the implementation of the exchange of information for the assessment of capital and

[102]Streinz, Europarecht, 9th ed. (C.F. Müller, 2012) § 6, para. 560.

[103]Haratsch, Koenig and Pechstein (Eds.), Europarecht, 9th ed. (Mohr Siebeck, 2014), 153 para. 347.

[104]Commission Delegated Regulation (EU) No 529/2014 of 12 March 2014 supplementing Regulation (EU) No 575/2013 of the European Parliament and of the Council with regard to regulatory technical standards for assessing the materiality of extensions and changes of the Internal Ratings Based Approach and the Advanced Measurement Approach.

liquidity.[105] In any case, the European Commission tries to strengthen its own role as delegated rule.[106]

As part of the programming of standards, within the organisation relationship the European Commission is involved with the European Parliament, Council and the European Banking Authority in information relations of vote, consultation and statement. In order to meet the developments in international financial markets, the legislation by the European Commission gains a high practical importance.

## 3.6 Model Type 4: Implementer

The model type of the *implementer* implements the control programmes and directly takes decisions on banking regulation immediately at national level in the Member States.

### *3.6.1 Characteristics*

The central organisation model in the field of banking regulation is the implementer. The legal basis for the establishment and enforcement measures of actors are both the primary and secondary European law and national laws. Purposes range from the maintenance of price stability to a contribution to the stability and effectiveness of the financial system, to the strengthening of the financial market through restructuring and reorganisation measures. These are independent regulators with collegial steering and quasi-judicial committees. Tasks include supervisory and resolution measures connected with powers to grant and withdraw authorisation of credit institutes, to request liquidity and solvency ratios; for the sale of the business, for the establishment of a bridge institution that act as intermediary, for asset separation or a bail-in of credit institutions. Of particular importance is the organisational relationship, as European enforcement powers limit the reach of the national enforcement powers, which shall be compensated by extensive information relations.

[105] Commission Implementing Regulation (EU) No 710/2014 of 23 June 2014 laying down implementing technical standards with regard to conditions of application of the joint decision process for institution-specific prudential requirements according to Directive 2013/36/EU.

[106] Gurlit, The ECB's relationship to EBA, Europäische Zeitschrift für Wirtschaftsrecht (2014), Supplement, 14 (17).

### 3.6.2 *Form of Appearance*

The form of appearance of the implementer can be found at European and at national level. In response to the fragmentation of the banking regulation, at European level, the European Central Bank was, as of 01.11.2014, entrusted with the Single Supervisory Mechanism and, as of 01.01.2015, the Single Resolution Mechanism with a coherent banking regulation. These actors at European level correspond to the Federal Financial Supervisory Authority and the Agency for Financial Stability at national level.

#### 3.6.2.1 European Central Bank (Single Supervisory Mechanism)

Together with the national supervisory authorities the European Central Bank (ECB) forms a Single Supervisory Mechanism (SSM). The Single Supervisory Mechanism is merely a mechanism and no separate European institution. Legal basis is Regulation (EU) No 1024/2013. As an institution of the European Union, the European Central Bank has its own legal personality. Furthermore, the European Central Bank under Art 130 TFEU and the Single Supervisory Mechanism under Art 19 of Regulation (EU) 1024/2013 act independently in their tasks. The aim of the Single Supervisory Mechanism is to ensure soundness of credit institutions, the stability of the financial system and the avoidance of regulatory arbitrage by a coherent banking supervision.[107] Organisationally, the Single Supervisory Mechanism is divided into a Single Supervisory Board[108] and a Steering Committee.[109] The Supervisory Board consists of one representative of each national supervisory authority of the euro States. It is the central decision-making body. The Single Supervisory Board has a quorum if two of its voting members are present. It decides by a simple majority of its members or, if it comes to the adoption of directly applicable regulations, with a weighting of votes, which corresponds with the voting rules for qualified majority voting in the Council of the European Union.[110]

The European Central Bank is solely responsible for all tasks in Art 4 (1) of Regulation (EU) No 1024/2013 regarding all credit institutions which have their seat in Member States participating in the Single Supervisory Mechanism. One limitation arises from Art 6 of Regulation (EU) No 1024/2013, which divides the supervision between the European Central Bank and the national supervisory authorities. Accordingly, the European Central Bank takes over the supervision of major financial institutions through joint supervisory teams, while less significant

---

[107]Art 1 subpara. 1 and Rec. 12, 15, 16, 20 of Regulation (EU) 1024/2013.

[108]Art 2-8 Rules of Procedure of the Supervisory Board of the European Central Bank.

[109]Art 9-12 Rules of Procedure of the Supervisory Board of the European Central Bank.

[110]Art 6.5 Rules of Procedure of the Supervisory Board of the European Central Bank.

institutions are still supervised by the national supervisory authorities.[111] The dissociation takes place with given parameters that shall illustrate the size, economic significance and the importance of cross-border activities.[112] Thus, the criteria may alternatively be satisfied, which means that already one requirement is sufficient to consider the credit institutes to be significant and to establish the authority of the European Central Bank.[113] The instruments of the European Central Bank range from mild (communication) to medium (warnings, recommendations) to hard powers to intervene.[114] In particular, the European Central Bank has comprehensive information, auditing and investigative powers, which also extend to cross-border banks or national supervised banks, each not considered to be significant.[115] Furthermore, the European Central Bank has comprehensive rights to be heard, consultation and statement rights in the area of banking regulation. This is followed by immediate competencies for regulations, guidelines or directives with respect to banks, which are subject to direct supervision, as well as a right to issue constructions with respect to less significant banks under national supervision, that is limited to general questions[116] and a right to issue constructions with respect to national supervisory authorities, which may include instructions for individual cases.[117] As a result, the European Central Bank can perform supervision against both, significant and non-significant financial institutions and intervene through immediate guidelines for credit institutions or as "supervisor of supervisors"[118] through instructions for the supervisory authorities.

The European Central Bank stands in an organisational relationship with international banking regulation actors, the European supervisory authorities, the European Systemic Risk Board and the national supervisory authorities of the Member States and other States.[119] The European Central bank can in particular demand all information from the national supervisory authorities of the Member States that are necessary for the

[111] Art 3-10; Art 96-100 of Regulation (EU) No 468/2014; for concrete information see König, Einheitlicher Aufsichtsmechanismus, BaFin-Journal 5/2014, 18 (19), of which in Germany exist 24 significant institutions und about 1650 less significant institutions.

[112] Art 6 (4) of Regulation (EU) 1024/2013; Art 39-72 of Regulation (EU) No 468/2014 with further interpretation Schuster, The banking supervisory competences and powers of the ECB, Europäische Zeitschrift für Wirtschaftsrecht (2014), Supplement, 3 (5).

[113] Deutsche Bundesbank, European Single Supervisory Mechanism for banks – a first step on the road to a banking union, 65 Monthly Report (2013) No. 7, 13 (15).

[114] Deutsche Bundesbank, Macroprudential Oversight in Germany: framework, institutions and tools, 65 Monthly Report (2013) No. 4, 39 (47).

[115] Art 9-12 of Regulation (EU) 1024/2013.

[116] Art 6 (4) and (5) lit. a) of Regulation (EU) 1024/2013.

[117] Art 6 (4) and (5) lit. b), Art 9 (1) subpara. 3 of Regulation (EU) 1024/2013, for different opinion see König, Einheitlicher Aufsichtsmechanismus, BaFin-Journal 5/2014, 18 (20).

[118] Schuster, The banking supervisory competences and powers of the ECB, Europäische Zeitschrift für Wirtschaftsrecht (2014), Supplement, 3 (6).

[119] Art 3 and 8 of Regulation (EU) 1024/2013.

supervision of credit institutes.[120] Furthermore, the national supervisory authorities are in favour of the European Central Bank to inform them about the initiation of essential supervisory measures and the issue of essential supervisory decisions.

#### 3.6.2.2 Single Resolution Board (Single Resolution Mechanism)

The Single Resolution Mechanism consists of the Single Resolution Board (SRB) and the Single Bank Resolution Fund. Legal basis for the Single Resolution Board is Regulation (EU) No 806/2014,[121] while the Single Resolution Fund is based on an international treaty.[122] The aim of the Single Resolution Mechanism is to prevent the socialisation of risks from banking transactions and losses emerging upon their realisation by first letting shareholders and obligees of the institution to bear any losses and relieve the taxpayer.[123] Furthermore, financing arrangements shall be established in form of a resolution fund.[124]

The Single Resolution Board is an independent European agency with its own legal personality.[125] The Committee is composed of a Chair, four further full-time members and one member appointed by each participating Member State, representing their national resolution authorities.[126] Organisationally, the committee is divided up into a plenary and an executive committee. All members of the board shall participate in the plenary sessions, while the executive session is composed of the Chair and the four full-time members.[127] Within the plenary sessions the decisions are taken by a simple majority of its members, also decisions on financial

---

[120] Art 6 (2) of Regulation (EU) 1024/2013.

[121] Regulation (EU) 806/2014 of the European Parliament and of the Council of 15 July 2014 establishing uniform rules and a uniform procedure for the resolution of credit institutions and certain investment firms in the framework of a Single Resolution Mechanism and a Single Resolution Fund.

[122] Intergovernmental Agreement on the transfer and mutualisation of contributions to the Single Resolution Fund of the Council of the European Union (8457/14), 14 May 2014; see short analysis of Wojcik and Ceyssens, Der einheitliche EU-Bankenabwicklungsmechanismus, Europäische Zeitschrift für Wirtschaftsrecht (2014), 893 (895).

[123] Deutsche Bundesbank, Europe's new recovery and resolution regime for credit institutions, 66 Monthly Report (2014) No. 6, 31 (44).

[124] National Resolution Funds according to Art 100 et seq. of Directive 2014/59/EU of the European Parliament and of the European Council of 15 May 2014 establishing a framework for the recovery and resolution of credit institutions and investment firms, OJ L 173, 12.06.2014, p. 190 are taken in by the Single Bank Resolution Fund. The Single Bank Resolution Fund is filled according to the rules agreed on in the Intergovernmental Agreement by the transfer of national funds, Art 67 (1) of Regulation (EU) No 806/2014. The Single Bank Resolution Fund is administered through the Single Resolution Board and can be consulted within the scope of the directive for the effective application of the resolution instruments, Art 75 (1), Art 76 (1)1 of Regulation (EU) No. 806/2014.

[125] Art 42, 47 of Regulation (EU) No 806/2014.

[126] Art 43 of Regulation (EU) No 806/2014.

[127] Art 49, 53 of Regulation (EU) No 806/2014.

means available in the Fund are taken by a simple majority of the Board members.[128] The tasks of the Single Resolution Board include the preparation of resolution plans,[129] the assessment of resolvability[130] of an institution as well as the preparation of concrete resolution decision.

In the case of financial difficulties of a financial institute, resolution authorities can carry out a recovery or resolution to avoid systemic risks and contagion effects on other market participants. This requires on the one hand the development of recovery plans by the credit institutes and, on the other hand, the creation of resolution plans for these institutions by the competent supervisory authority.[131] The recovery process is performed in ownership of the credit institution. This assumes that the credit institute set up a recovery plan to be prepared in case of need and to be able to fall back on existing concepts.[132] In order to draw up a resolution plan, the credit institutes need to provide information for the resolution authorities in order to draw up institute-specific or group-specific detailed resolution plans, to obtain the functions and core business areas.[133] In addition, the Single Resolution Board has extensive powers, ranging from information requests, to examinations and to on-site inspections.[134] There are also extensive powers for early intervention by supervisory authorities.[135] At the opening of a resolution procedure, three conditions must be met[136]: The entity is failing or is likely to fail; having regard to timing and other relevant circumstances, there is no reasonable prospect that any alternative private sector measures would prevent its failure within a reasonable timeframe; a resolution action is necessary in the public interest. If these conditions for a resolution are met and a resolution procedure has been initiated, the resolution authority has several instruments[137]: the resolution tools include the sale of the business,[138] the establishment of a bridge institution,[139] the asset separation[140] and a bail-in.[141]

---

[128]Art 52 (1) and (2) of Regulation (EU) No 806/2014.

[129]Art 8 and 9 of Regulation (EU) No. 806/2014.

[130]Art 10-12 of Regulation (EU) No. 806/2014.

[131]Waschbusch and Rolle, Testament von Banken. Sanierungs- und Abwicklungspläne im Rahmen aktueller Reformprozesse, Wirtschafswissenschaftliches Studium, 42 (2013), 453 (454).

[132]Art 5-9 of Directive 2014/59/EU.

[133]Art 10, 11 of Directive 2014/59/EU.

[134]Art 34-36 of Regulation (EU) No. 806/2014.

[135]Art 13 of Regulation (EU) No. 806/2014; Art 27-29 of Directive 2014/59/EU.

[136]Art 18 (1) lit. a)- c), paras. 2-10 of Regulation (EU) No. 806/2014.

[137]Art 16 (1), Art 22 (2), 24-27 of Regulation (EU) No. 806/2014.

[138]A sale of the business is any sovereign disposal activities to another institution by the resolution authority.

[139]The establishment of a bridge institution serves the maintenance of critical functions.

[140]In contrast, the separation of assets in a special purpose vehicle serves not just the continuation of critical functions, but the subsequent purchase.

[141]A bail-in is a direct loss absorbency by the investor, comparable Art 48a et seq. German Banking Act; a bail-out as ultima ratio is a measure by the government to stable a credit institute, which is foreseen in Art 56 et seq. BRRD, but not adopted in Regulation (EU) No. 806/2014.

The Single Resolution has not only with the national resolution authorities a narrow organisational relationship, but also with the European Commission and the Council. The national resolution authorities are consulted and can participate, while the European Commission and the Council shall be informed by the scope of a bank resolution.[142]

#### 3.6.2.3 Federal Financial Supervisory Authority

The Federal Financial Supervisory Authority (BaFin) was established on the basis of Art 87 (4) sentence 1 of the German Basic Law as a direct federal, public-law institution.[143] The organs of the Federal Financial Supervisory Authority are the Executive Board, the President and the Administrative Council.[144] The Executive Board[145] has as a collegial body the overall responsibility for managing the Federal Financial Supervisory Authority, Art 6 (1) sentence 1 and 2 Act Establishing the Federal Financial Supervisory Authority.[146] Decisions of the Executive Board are taken by a simple majority of the votes cast Art 6 (2) sentence 1 Act Establishing the Federal Financial Supervisory Authority. In case of a tie, the President has the casting vote.[147] The Administrative Council is responsible for the management of the Federal Financial Supervisory Authority. It consists of two further representatives of the Federal Ministry of Finance, one representative of the Federal Ministry of Economics and Technology, one representative of the Federal Ministry of Justice, five members of the Bundestag, five representatives of the credit institutions, four representatives of the insurance undertakings and one representative of the asset management companies.[148]

One of the central tasks of the Federal Financial Supervisory Authority is the sovereign supervision of credit institutions, which are not significant in the sense of Regulation (EU) 1024/2013. According to Art 6 (3) German Banking Act it is empowered to take appropriate and necessary measures for banks in individual cases. Next to the Federal Financial Supervisory Authority, the Deutsche Bundesbank

[142]Art 30-32, Art 45 of Regulation (EU) No. 806/2014.

[143]Art 1 (1) Finanzdienstleistungsaufsichtsgesetz (FinDAG = Act Establishing the Federal Financial Supervisory Authority), as published in the announcement of 22 April 2002 (Federal Law Gazette I p. 1310), last amended 6 December 2011 (Federal Law Gazette I, p. 2481).

[144]Art 5 (1) Act Establishing the Federal Financial Supervisory Authority.

[145]Consists of one President and four Chief Executive Directors for banking supervision, securities supervision, insurance supervision and cross-sectional tasks/ internal administration.

[146]For expert advice Advisory Boards can be created (Art 8, 8a) or third parties (e.g. auditors) can be used to accomplish tasks (Art 4 (3) Act Establishing the Federal Financial Supervisory Authority).

[147]Art 6 (2) sentence 2, the President has policy-making powers for the strategic orientation of the integrated financial supervision, that examines the relationship of the President to the Executive Directors (Art 6 (3) Act Establishing the Federal Financial Supervisory Authority).

[148]Art 7 (3) Act Establishing the Federal Financial Supervisory Authority.

carries out the ongoing supervision of institutions, in accordance with Art 7 German Banking Act.[149] With the ongoing supervision[150] the Bundesbank carries out the quantitative supervisory and undertakes preparatory work for administrative acts and general orders of the Federal Financial Supervisory Authority. The Federal Financial Supervisory Authority carries out the qualitative supervision on the basis of audit findings and assessments of the Bundesbank[151] with the help of the event-based or rotational adoption of regulatory measures against a credit institution.[152] To enforce the supervisory rights,[153] the Federal Financial Supervisory Authority regularly uses instruments of the administrative act.[154] In addition, it also operates through general supervisory activities (cautions, exhortations) or informal measures (talks), which are legally non-binding but effective in practice (moral persuasion) as simple administrative action.[155]

The Federal Financial Supervisory Authority operates with the Deutsche Bundesbank in an organisational relationship with information relations regarding the supervision of credit institutions. Here, the flow of information runs from the Bundesbank to the Federal Financial Supervisory Authority.[156] Furthermore, the Federal Financial Supervisory Authority is regularly in an organisational relationship with the Deutsche Bundesbank with rights of consultation, advisory and statement to the European Banking Authority, the Single Supervisory Board, the European Central Bank, the Basel Committee on Banking Supervision and the Financial Stability Board.

[149]The embodiment for the organisational purpose of the banking supervision equals according to Art 7 German Banking Act a hermaphrodite construction between the Federal Financial Supervisory Authority and the Deutsche Bundesbank, see Höfling, Gutachten zum 68. Deutschen Juristentag, (C.H. Beck, 2010), F46; the reason lies in Art 87 (3) GG, whereby the federal government gets the possibility of establishing the Federal Financial Supervisory Authority, but the establishment of the administrative infrastructure for a higher federal authority is denied, BVerfGE 14, 197 (210 et seq.); this is followed by the integration of the Deutsche Bundesbank. The interaction shall also help the administrative economics, since the Bundesbank maintains a further branch network, which is missing within Federal Financial Supervisory Authority, it can supervise credit institutions locally, Schäfer, in Boos/Fischer/Schulte-Mattler (Eds.), KWG, 4th ed. (C.H. Beck, 2012), § 7 para. 5.

[150]Assessment of the documents submitted by the institutions, evaluation of audit reports, analysis of the annual financial statements, implementation and evaluation of the banking business audits for the assessment of capital adequacy and risk management, see Schäfer, in Boos/Fischer/Schulte-Mattler (Eds.), KWG, 4th ed. (C.H. Beck, 2012), § 7 para. 20.

[151]Schäfer, in Boos/Fischer/Schulte-Mattler (Eds.), KWG, 4th ed. (C.H. Beck, 2012), § 7, para. 39.

[152]Schäfer, in Boos/Fischer/Schulte-Mattler (Eds.), KWG, 4th ed. (C.H. Beck, 2012), § 6 para. 5.

[153]In particular based on the legal basis of § 6 (2) and (3), § 35 (2), § 45, § 56 and § 60 German Banking Act.

[154]Schäfer, in Boos/Fischer/Schulte-Mattler (Eds.), KWG, 4th ed. (C.H. Beck, 2012), § 6 para. 9.

[155]Schäfer, in Boos/Fischer/Schulte-Mattler (Eds.), KWG, 4th ed. (C.H. Beck, 2012), § 6 paras. 15, 23.

[156]Schäfer, in Boos/Fischer/Schulte-Mattler (Eds.), KWG, 4th ed. (C.H. Beck, 2012), § 7 para. 8.

#### 3.6.2.4 Federal Agency for Financial Market Stabilisation

The Federal Agency for Financial Market Stabilisation is a legally dependent institution under public law, which may act in its own name, but is subject to the legal and technical supervision of the Federal Ministry of Finance.[157] Purpose of the institution is the administration of the resolution fund.[158] Central decision-making body is a Steering Committee composed of three members, which shall act by an absolute majority.[159] Its main tasks are, as of 01.01.2015, the administration and decision-making over the resources of the restructuring fund in cooperation with the Single Resolution Board after the information exchange with the Federal Financial Supervisory Authority.

## 3.7 Model Type 5: Controller

The last model type is the *controller* who examines and evaluates the decisions and measures of bank regulators; it also carries out a general monitoring of the implementation of the legal framework of banking regulation.

### *3.7.1 Characteristics*

The last organisational model of regulatory actors is the controller. The respective actors carry out a monitoring of the implementation of the regulation and the decisions of the regulatory framework at a national level. The actors at the international level have only limited authority for monitoring or observation due to weak institutional arrangements without formal decision-making bodies. They only have an indirectly moral, but not a direct legally binding influence on regulatory measures. In contrast, the European players have the competence to correct or sanction possible forces of misregulations due to the European treaties or the European secondary legislation with the help of complex decision-making bodies. Although there are organisational relationships between the respective actors, the effectiveness of these information relations for comprehensive and timely prevention of crises in practice can yet not be reviewed.

[157]Art 1 Verordnung über die Satzung der Bundesanstalt für Finanzmarktstabilisierung (FMSA-SatzV = Statute of the Federal Agency for Financial Market Stabilisation) as published in the announcement of 21 February 2011 (Federal Law Gazette I p. 272), last amended 20 December 2012 (Federal Law Gazette I, p. 2777).

[158]Art 2 (1) Statute of the Federal Agency for Financial Market Stabilisation.

[159]Art 4 (1), Art 5 (1) and (3) Statute of the Federal Agency for Financial Market Stabilisation.

## 3.7.2 *Form of Appearance*

The form of appearance of the controller at international and European level focuses primarily on a macro-prudential supervision, which in turn allows conclusions on the micro-prudential level.

### 3.7.2.1 European Central Bank

The European Central Bank may over the Single Supervisory Mechanism[160] also impose administrative sanctions to credit institutes for breaching regulatory requirements in accordance with Article 18 of Regulation (EU) No. 1024/2013. Alternatively, the national supervisory authority may be advised. The organisational relationships and information relations bring the European Central Bank enormous power of action and a huge amount of information, which can lead to a direct control of the national credit institutes while skipping the national supervisory authorities, in order to ensure the implementation of regulatory requirements and measures in the event of a crisis.

### 3.7.2.2 European Banking Authority

The European Banking Authority[161] as a European Union agency undertakes peer-reviews with its Working Groups to promote the coherence within the network of financial supervisors. With the help of national supervisory authorities, the Board of Supervisors decides on the frame method for the assessment of the work of the supervisory authorities in order to bring the ability of the supervisory authority in line. The results can be published after being approved by the inspected authority.[162] This interplay of publication after approval is due to the organisational relationships of the European Banking Authority.

### 3.7.2.3 Basel Committee on Banking Supervision

The Basel Committee on Banking Supervision[163] takes after its mandate also the supervision of the implementation of the standards in member countries and beyond to ensure their timely, consistent and effective implementation and to contribute to the adoption of the same rules for all internationally active banks.[164] However, this

[160]See details at 3.4.2.1.

[161]See details at 3.6.2.1.

[162]Rec. 41 of Regulation (EU) No 1093/2010.

[163]See details at 3.3.2.2.

[164]Art 2 lit. e) Basel Committee on Banking Supervision Charter.

task has exclusively political effect, since the Basel Committee has no powers to enforce or sanction of a missing, incomplete or delayed implementation. The only thing left is moral persuasion.

#### 3.7.2.4 International Monetary Fund

The International Monetary Fund is an International Governmental Organisation that was created under an international treaty within the United Nations. The Fund consists currently of 188 members.[165] The members represent states but neither national institutions such as central banks or regulatory agencies nor supranational organisations.[166] The main aim of the International Monetary Fund is financial assistance and guidance in surveillance.[167] To pursue these aims the Fund operates with a slim organisational structure consisting of the Board of Governors, the Executive Board and the Managing Director.[168] The Board of Governors comprises of one governor and one alternate of each member state. This is usually the minister of finance or the governor of the national central bank.[169] The Board of Governors is the main decision-making body, whereas the Executive Board is responsible for conducting the business of the Fund.

The Fund monitors the international monetary system to ensure its effective functioning and monitors whether the members are in endeavour to direct its economic and financial policies toward the objective of fostering orderly economic growth with reasonable price stability.[170] Furthermore, the International Monetary Fund designs a so-called Financial Sector Assessment Programme for monitoring amongst others the unification of the regulatory framework and the regulatory parameters.[171] This soft law is legally non-binding, but only morally binding. The setting of macro-prudential best practice guidelines for information requirements and monitoring is an option to coordinate the national financial systems. Though, it is not enough to ensure an effective global surveillance. The International Monetary Fund cannot yet play its role as a key player in the "international concert of financial institutions".[172]

---

[165] International Monetary Fund – The IMF at a Glance (available online, last downloaded 28.02.2015 at http://www.imf.org/external/np/exr/facts/glance.htm).

[166] Manger-Nestler, Interaction for Monetary and Financial Stability, in Hermann, Krajewski and Terhechte (Eds.), European Yearbook of International Economic Law, Vol. 5 (2014), 33 (44).

[167] Art I IMF Articles of Agreement.

[168] Art XII Section 1 IMF Articles of Agreement.

[169] Manger-Nestler, Interaction for Monetary and Financial Stability, in Hermann, Krajewski and Terhechte (Eds.), European Yearbook of International Economic Law, Vol. 5 (2014), 33 (45).

[170] Art IV Section 3 lit.a in conjunction with Art IV Section 1 IMF Articles of Agreement.

[171] Grande, Banking Regulation and supervision – developments and prospects at the global and EU levels, in Grieser and Heemann (Eds.), Bankenaufsichtsrecht, (Frankfurt School Verlag, 2010), 19 (31).

[172] Manger-Nestler, Interaction for Monetary and Financial Stability, in Hermann, Krajewski and Terhechte (Eds.), European Yearbook of International Economic Law, Vol. 5 (2014), 33 (49).

## 3.8 Conclusion: Consequences for the Influence of Organisations on Decisions

The influence of organisations on the decision-making process largely depends on the underlying institutional arrangements. They determine in particular the principles of organisation and the decision-making process, the competencies and information relations that are crucial in a multi-polar association of administration. Because of common structures, organisational models can be formed and systematise the actors of banking regulation.

# Chapter 4
# Theses About the Organisation of Banking Regulations

The organisation of banking regulation concerns the supervision and resolution of banks. As a result of the financial and banking crisis, the legal framework was tightened at a European and national level. Therewith, extensive tasks and competencies were created at a European level to counteract the fragmentation of the national regulatory law as well as a different supervisory and resolution practice. Banking supervision and banking resolution are now done in the European Composite Administration. Specifically, the Banking supervision shifts further to the European level due to the European Central Bank, while the bank resolution still remains on the national level at the Federal Agency for Financial Market Stabilisation. Changes in the banking regulatory architecture lead to tension with the principles of the state under the rule of law and democracy (theses 1, 3, 4 and 5). In particular, within the European Central Bank the centralisation of competences collides with the stated object of the primary law of monetary policy to maintain price stability (thesis 2). Furthermore, the normative foundations of regulatory actors determine the power of each administrative organisation and its influence on regulatory decisions (Thesis 6 and 7).

## 4.1 Banking Regulation Follows no Legal Foundation in the European Treaties

According to Art 2 TEU, the principle of the rule of law is one of the values of the European Union. One element of the rule of law is the legality of the administration. These include the priority and the reservation of the law. The priority of the law stipulates that the administration must not violate the law with its actions. The reservation of the law rather determines that every action of the administration must be done on a legal basis.[1] For the area of banking regulation this means that banking supervision and resolution require a legal basis at European level. Member

[1]The legislative power of the community has to move in line with its contracts and is subject to the priority of the standards contained therein, Oppermann, Classen and Nettesheim (Eds.), Europarecht, 6th ed. (C.H. Beck, 2014), Art 11 (4); ECJ, C-106/77 of 09.03.1978 – Simmenthal [1978], ECR I- 626 = Neue Juristische Wochenschrift (1978), 1741.



A. Wellerdt, *Organisation of Banking Regulation*, SpringerBriefs in Law,
DOI 10.1007/978-3-319-17638-3_4

States, whose currency is the euro, carry out banking supervision on the basis of the Single Supervisory Mechanism, which was established organisationally in the European Central Bank. The measures of the European Central Bank are complemented by the European Banking Authority, which develops technical regulatory and implementing standards for all Member States of the European Union. In Euro Member States, the bank resolution is transmitted to the Single Resolution Board together with the national resolution authorities.

## *4.1.1 Legal Basis for a Banking Supervision by the European Central Bank*

The competence of the European Central Bank in terms of banking supervision results from Regulation (EU) No 1024/2013. Legal basis for the adoption of this Regulation is Art 127 (6) TFEU. Thereafter, the Council may unanimously act by means of the regulation "confer specific tasks upon the European Central Bank concerning policies relating to the prudential supervision of credit institutions and other financial institutions with the exception of insurance undertakings". It is questionable whether herein lies a legal basis for banking supervision. Useful for the understanding of the normative text is the legal interpretation.[2] For this purpose, four interpretation rules are applied: starting with the grammatical interpretation of the wording, followed by an interpretation of the historical origins and the systematic context and finally considering the sense and purpose of the norm.

### 4.1.1.1 Art 127 (6) TFEU

The wording of Art 127 (6) TFEU speaks of "specific tasks". The reference to "special" tasks suggests that the authorisation to confer only relates to individual supervisory tasks. This cannot subsume comprehensive supervisory responsibilities or supervision as a whole with drastic instruments.[3] Conversely, this would mean that the national supervisory authorities would only be responsible for the supervision of non-systemically important banks, for combating money laundering and for consumer protection. National supervisory authorities would be responsible for marginal tasks, while a nearly extensive supervisory competence of the European Central Bank is founded. The transfer of "special" tasks is exhausted. Not only marginal tasks, but also basic core tasks are transferred upon the European Central Bank. The wording empowered to confer "tasks" or functions of supervision, which does not include

[2]Larenz, Methodenlehre der Rechtswissenschaft, 6th ed. (Springer, 1991), 204.

[3]Kämmerer, Bahn frei der Bankenunion, Neue Zeitschrift für Verwaltungsrecht (2013), 830 (832 et seq.), for other opinion see Ceyssens Teufelskreis zwischen Banken und Staatsfinanzen – Der Europäische Bankaufsichtsmechanimus, Neue Juristische Wochenschrift (2013), 3704 (3706).

original competencies.[4] Such would be created with the banking supervision through the European Central Bank. Further, conferring special tasks needs to be "relating to" the supervision. What relation to means, is hard to define. Nevertheless, it can be concluded that the supervision itself cannot be the subject of a transfer.[5] As a result, the wording is to be interpreted strictly, since it clearly speaks against entrusting the European Central Bank with extensive decision-making powers, and against the creation of a central banking supervision.[6] This interpretation of the various components of the wording is underlined by the historical development of the norm. During the negotiations of the Treaty of Maastricht, central bank governors urged the European Central Bank to participate in banking supervision. The Member States rejected this claim. As a compromise, Art 105 (6) of the Treaty establishing the European Community (Art 127 (6) TFEU) was introduced, which tied the banking supervision by the European Central Bank just to the restrictive condition that the Council unanimously agrees to the participation of the European Central Bank.[7] Among the impressions of the banking crisis, the position of the Member States might have changed, but even the negotiations on the Treaty of Lisbon lead to no other historical interpretation. Art 127 TFEU is systematically in the chapter "Monetary Policy". Art 127 (1) TFEU names the price stability as primary objective of the European System of Central Banks. According to Art 127 (2) TFEU supervision does not belong to the basic tasks of the European System of Central Banks. According to Art 127 (5) TFEU the European System of Central Banks has the task "to the smooth conduct of policies pursued by the competent authorities relating to the prudential supervision of credit institutions and the stability of the financial system." To contribute to the implementation can thus not establish own competencies of the European Central Bank for banking supervision.[8] It follows that the banking supervision in the standard norm of Art 127 TFEU plays a subordinate role in relation to the monetary policy.[9] According to sense and purpose of Art 127 TFEU, banking supervision is not per se subjected to the European Central Bank and after Art 127 (6) TFEU, the banking supervision cannot be conferred as a whole.[10]

---

[4]Herdegen, Europäische Bankenunion, Wertpapiermitteilungen (2012), 1889 (1891).

[5]Kämmerer, Bahn frei der Bankenunion, Neue Zeitschrift für Verwaltungsrecht (2013), 830 (833 et seq.).

[6]Concurring, but critical Schuster, The banking supervisory competences and powers of the ECB, Europäische Zeitschrift für Wirtschaftsrecht (2014), Supplement, 3 (3); Wolfers and Voland, Europäische Zentralbank und Bankenaufsicht, Zeitschrift für Bank- und Kapitalmarktrecht (2014), 177 (179); Herdegen, Europäische Bankenunion, Wertpapiermitteilungen (2012), 1889 (1892).

[7]Glatzl, Geldpolitik und Bankenaufsicht im Konflikt, (Nomos, 2009), 257.

[8]Häde, Jenseits der Effizienz: Wer kontrolliert die Kontrolleure? Europäische Zeitschrift für Wirtschaftsrecht (2011), 662.

[9]Manger-Nestler, Interaction for Monetary and Financial Stability, in Hermann, Krajewski and Terhechte (Eds.), European Yearbook of International Economic Law, Vol. 5 (2014), 33 (44); Sacarcelik, Europäische Bankenunion, Zeitschrift für Bank- und Kapitalmarktrecht (2013), 353 (356).

[10]Kämmerer, Das neue Europäische Finanzaufsichtssystem (ESFS) – Modell für eine europäisierte Verwaltungsarchitektur, Neue Zeitschrift für Verwaltungsrecht (2011), 1281 (1283).

The interpretation leads to the conclusion that a banking supervision conducted by the European Central Bank cannot be based on the legal basis of Art 127 (6) TFEU. Possibly, authorising the European Central Bank to banking supervision—differing from the wording of the Regulation (EU) No 1024/2013—can be obtained in accordance with Art 114 TFEU or Art 352 TFEU to guarantee the legitimacy of the administration.

#### 4.1.1.2 Art 114 TFEU

On the basis of Art 114 TFEU the Union legislator may adopt measures for the approximation of legal and administrative regulations of the Member States in order to strengthen the conditions for the establishment and functioning of the internal market. The aim of Art 114 TFEU is the elimination of obstacles in the internal market resulting from the different legal systems of the Member States. The question is whether the re-establishment of sovereign powers of the European Union falls under *measurements for the approximation of the laws and regulations*. A justification of sovereign powers can only be founded on Art 114 TFEU as a special exception when they serve as an annex to the alignment and if thereby a significant added value for the internal market can be expected.[11] Even if a uniform banking supervision should be in favour of the internal market, due to the transfer of the banking supervision to the European Central Bank, a competence is justified before the laws and regulations have been adjusted for banking supervision.[12] Under approximation of legislation falls only the approximation with reference to relevant issues of national legal standards to a union legal standard in order to avoid national legal differences and thus potential distortions of competition.[13] With the establishment of the European Banking Authority the administrative powers of the European Union have been enhanced to ensure the stability of the financial system.[14] Systematic is to notice that, when a transfer of specific tasks can be only done by unanimous vote in the Council, Art 114 TFEU would annul this primary law restriction with the ordinary legislative procedure. It requires an independent legal basis. Art 127 (6) TFEU is lex specialis to Art 114 TFEU.[15] In addition, a uniform banking supervision detects only the euro states. Hence, a union-wide

---

[11]Herdegen, Europäische Bankenunion, Wertpapiermitteilungen (2012), 1889 (1891); Kahl, in Callies and Ruffert (Eds.), EUV/AEUV Commentary, (C.H. Beck, 2012), paras. 9, 20, 24 et seq.

[12]Recital (12) und (13) of Regulation (EU) No 1093 / 2010 show apparently that the Single Supervisory Mechanism shall focus on protecting the stability of the financial system instead of creating common conditions for financial market competition.

[13]Kahl, in Callies and Ruffert (Eds.), EUV/AEUV Commentary, (C.H. Beck, 2012), Art 114, para. 13.

[14]Eriksson, Einheitlicher Europäischer Bankenaufsichtsmechanismus, Wissenschaftliche Dienste, 2013, 32 (available online, last downloaded 28.02.2015 at https://www.bundestag.de/blob/194116/1b35853890a67f88b660d07278354a9c/bankenaufsichtsmechanismus-data.pdf).

[15]Kämmerer, Bahn frei der Bankenunion, Neue Zeitschrift für Verwaltungsrecht (2013), 830 (835).

harmonisation of the laws and regulations is just not possible. Such an interpretation would contradict the sense and purpose of the norm. Rather, the union-wide harmonisation is in the responsibility of the European Banking Authority in cooperation with the European Commission due to the development of technical regulatory and implementing standards.

#### 4.1.1.3 Art 352 TFEU

The objectives of Art 352 TFEU authorises the European Union to take action to attain one of the objectives set out in the Treaties if the Treaties have not provided the necessary power. The wording of the norm is defined very broadly and is likely to be interpreted restrictively, to provide no "blanket powers" to take action.[16] Art 127 (6) TFEU authorises only the transmission of specific tasks for establishing a standardised banking supervision. The delegation of powers is not explicitly mentioned. The scope of Art 352 TFEU could be opened.[17] The establishment of an internal market is in accordance with Art 3 (3) sentence 1 TEU one of the objectives of the European Union. However, the creation of a standardised banking supervision by the European Central Bank comprises only the Member States whose currency is the euro. Thus, the internal market for financial services would not be standardised, but rather fragmented. In addition, the standardised banking supervision by the European Central Bank would be longer a supplement, but an extension of competences already part of the contract so that Art 352 TFEU is ruled out to be a legal basis.[18]

### *4.1.2 Legal Basis for a Banking Regulation by the European Banking Authority*

For the establishment of the European Banking Authority the Regulation (EU) No 1093/2010 on the basis of Art 114 TFEU serves as a legal basis. The establishment of the European Banking Authority should, however, be related to the approximation of legal regulations and regulatory provisions. The establishment of the European Banking Authority serves less for a harmonisation of law, but for an extension of legal powers.[19] The problem is that the European Banking Authority

[16]Sacarcelik, Europäische Bankenunion, Zeitschrift für Bank- und Kapitalmarktrecht (2013), 353 (356).

[17]For other opinion see Herdegen, Europäische Bankenunion, Wertpapiermitteilungen (2012), 1889 (1892), regards Art 127 (6) TFEU as final and rules out a recourse to Art 352 TFEU dispositive powers and flexibility clause.

[18]Herdegen, Europäische Bankenunion, Wertpapiermitteilungen (2012), 1889 (1892).

[19]Häde, Jenseits der Effizienz: Wer kontrolliert die Kontrolleure? Europäische Zeitschrift für Wirtschaftsrecht (2011), 662 (663).

cannot only coordinate but also discipline or replace the national supervisory authorities in certain areas. In individual cases, the European Banking Authority can, based on the regular tasks of Art 8 in Regulation (EU) No 1093/2010, claim proceedings, disempower national authorities in the course of continuing infringements of rights and intervene in crisis situations or conflicts between national supervisory authorities.[20] Such far-reaching rights to intervene of a European authority against national competent authorities are comparable with the provisions in Art 11 (6) of Regulation (EU) No 1/2003 on the procedure of the European Commission in competition law. However, there is a crucial difference between the specific regulatory law for banks and the general competition law. According to Art 3 TFEU, the European Union is responsible for establishing the competition rules necessary for the functioning of the internal market. Regulation (EU) No 1/2003 regulates the administrative procedure in competition law, which is enforced by the European Commission. In contrast, the banking regulation does not fall under the exclusive competence to regulate monetary policy in the Member States whose currency is the euro. Consequently, the European Union shares competencies with the Member States in the field of banking regulation. A standardisation of the administrative procedures has not yet taken place in the field of banking supervision and resolution. The result is that the competencies of the European Banking Authority go beyond the legal basis. Moreover, it is questionable whether the establishment of the European Banking Authority limits are already set by the European Court of Justice in the Meroni case. These decisions limited the delegation of powers of the European Union to authorities.[21] The European Union is only allowed to transmit clearly defined executive powers. Powers which have to be exercised at one's own discretion and require wide discretionary powers that cannot be transferred.[22] In particular, greater powers than conferred upon the European Union by the Treaty are generally not to be transmitted through secondary legislation on a European authority.[23] Exceptionally, however, policy-relevant powers can be conferred to new facilities by secondary legislation when the power shift holds "balance of powers".[24] According to Regulation (EU) No 1093/2010 the European Banking Authority only receives indirect competencies to develop technical regulatory and implementing standards that are adopted by the European Union. However, in individual cases, it also has its own powers to intervene.[25] It is questionable whether this power shift is within in the "balance of powers". A decision could be left open when the principles of the Meroni case are not directly applicable.

[20] Art 17 (4) and (6), Art 18 (4) and (5), Art 19 (4) and (5) of Regulation (EU) No.1093/2010.
[21] ECJ 9/56, ECR 1958, p.9 (11); ECJ 10/56, ECR 1958, 53 (81) – Meroni / High Commission.
[22] ECJ 9/56, ECR 1958, p.9 (44); ECJ 10/56, ECR 1958, 53 (81) – Meroni / High Commission.
[23] ECJ 9/56, ECR 1958, p.9 (40); ECJ 10/56, ECR 1958, 53 (79) – Meroni / High Commission.
[24] ECJ 9/56, ECR 1958, p.9 (44) – Meroni / High Commission.
[25] Comparable with the competencies of the European Commission in the competition law.

The decision of the European Court of Justice in the Meroni case refers to the delegation of existing powers by the European Commission. It is not exactly a shift of existing powers of the European Commission, but a justification of new competences for the European Union.[26] The European Banking Authority undertakes tasks that hitherto no body of the European Union was entitled to, but authorities of the Member States.[27] In addition, only the development of technical standards is delegated to the European Banking Authority, while the European Commission has to adopt drafts before they have indirect effect as decision. It follows that the principles of the Meroni case cannot be directly transferred on the establishment of the European Banking Authority.

As a result, the establishment of the European Banking Authority is compatible with the unwritten principles of European judicial decisions, while the equipment with powers goes beyond the legal basis of Art 114 TFEU in particular cases.

### *4.1.3 Legal Basis for a Bank Resolution*

The recovery and resolution of banks is assigned to a Single Resolution Mechanism due to Regulation (EU) No 806/2014 on the basis of Art 114 TFEU. The problem is that the establishment of the Single Resolution Mechanism serves less for a legislative approximation as an expansion of legal powers. Moreover, it is again questionable, whether the creation of the Single Resolution Board is compatible with the principles of the European Court of Justice in the Meroni case. Accordingly, the European Union can only confer clearly defined executive powers, while powers that have to be exercised at one's own discretion are not to be transferred.[28] The Single Resolution Board is designed as a European agency with its own legal personality. It has extensive investigative powers and decides on the resolution of all banks under the supervision of the Single Supervisory Mechanism of the European Central Bank, of other banks with subsidiaries in other participating Member States, and if Member States have transferred competencies. In all other cases the power for rehabilitation and resolution remains with the national resolution authorities. In addition, greater powers than conferred upon the European Union by the Treaty are generally not to be transmitted through secondary legislation on a European authority.[29] A restriction was made in the recent judgements of the European Court of Justice with regard to the European Securities and

[26] Sacarcelik, Europäische Bankenunion, Zeitschrift für Bank- und Kapitalmarktrecht (2013), 353 (356); Häde, Jenseits der Effizienz: Wer kontrolliert die Kontrolleure? Europäische Zeitschrift für Wirtschaftsrecht (2011), 662 (663), Herdegen Banking Supervision within the European Union, (De Gruyter, 2010), 57 et seq.

[27] Häde, Jenseits der Effizienz: Wer kontrolliert die Kontrolleure? Europäische Zeitschrift für Wirtschaftsrecht (2011), 662 (663).

[28] ECJ 9/56, ECR 1958, p.9 (44); ECJ 10/56, ECR 1958, 53 (81) – Meroni / High Commission.

[29] ECJ 9/56, ECR 1958, p.9 (40); ECJ 10/56, ECR 1958, 53 (79) – Meroni / High Commission.

Markets Authority.[30] Accordingly, a Union legislator is exceptionally authorised to create Union authorities with limited powers, if one considers such a decision necessary. On the one hand, possible measures of the Single Resolution Board require specific expertise in an appropriate reaction time.[31] On the other hand, wide ranging investigation and decision powers are granted to the Single Resolution Board involving the European Commission and the Council. It is questionable whether this involvement does justice to the decision requirements of Meroni as well as to the European Securities and Markets Authority. Firstly, the European Commission and the Council are only authorised limited to control resolution decisions. Secondly, a regular involvement in temporary decisions in times of crisis in order to enable capacity to act appears doubtful.

The decision of the European Court of Justice in the Meroni case refers to the delegation of existing powers by the European Commission.[32] It is not exactly a shift of existing powers of the European Commission, but a justification of new competences for the European Union. The result of which is that the principles of the Meroni case cannot be directly transferred on the establishment of the European Banking Authority.

The creation of the single European Resolution Board as a European agency goes beyond the legal basis of Art 114 TFEU and appears difficult to reconcile with the unwritten principles of European judicial decisions.

### *4.1.4 Interim Result for the Legal Basis of Banking Regulation*

Banking supervision by the Single Supervisory Mechanism in the European Central Bank cannot be based on the legal basis of Art 127 (6); 114 or 352 TFEU. The wording of Art 127 (6) TFEU is too tight, the transfer of powers to the European Central Bank in accordance with Art 114 TFEU goes beyond the guarantee of standardised supervisory standards and a rounding of the Treaty according to Art 352 TFEU does not cover any extension of competences. The European Central Bank may only exercise such legislative decision or exercise executive powers, to

[30]ECJ Decision of 22.01.2014, C 270/12 = Neue Juristische Wochenschrift (2014), 1359 – United Kingdom Great Britain and North Ireland / European Parliament and Council of the European Union; differing view Wojcik and Ceyssens, Der einheitliche EU-Bankenabwicklungsmechanismus, Europäische Zeitschrift für Wirtschaftsrecht (2014), 893 (897).

[31]Deutsche Bundesbank, Europe's new recovery and resolution regime for credit institutions, 66 Monthly Report (2014) No.6, 48.

[32]Sacarcelik, Europäische Bankenunion, Zeitschrift für Bank- und Kapitalmarktrecht (2013), 353 (356); Häde, Jenseits der Effizienz: Wer kontrolliert die Kontrolleure? Europäische Zeitschrift für Wirtschaftsrecht (2011), 662 (664), Herdegen Banking Supervision within the European Union, (De Gruyter, 2010), 57 et seq.; with other arguments Wojcik and Ceyssens, Der einheitliche EU-Bankenabwicklungsmechanismus, Europäische Zeitschrift für Wirtschaftsrecht (2014), 893 (895).

which it was entitled to by primary legislation. An explicit task assignment for banking regulation as a crisis management is missing.[33] Thus crisis management relevant for financial markets is not an inherent task of a central bank that could establish an authorisation. Banking Supervision as core of banking regulation lacks a legal basis. A standardisation and specification of banking regulation through technical implementation and regulatory standards of the European Banking Authority and the European Commission cannot be based on Art 114 TFEU, however, is still compatible with the principles of the European Court of Justice in the Meroni case. Bank resolution as counterpart of banking supervision as European agency in the form of the Single Resolution Board cannot be based on Art 114 TFEU and is only compatible with the unwritten principles of European judicial decisions due to a benevolent interpretation.

As a result, measures of banking regulation lack appropriate legal bases. Rather, the lack of a legal basis cannot be cured through a majority for the adoption of a national Approval Act within the sense of Art 23 (1) German Basic Law.[34] In addition, the Federal Constitutional Court of Germany could control the Approval Law. The Federal Constitutional Court of Germany has already stated in the Maastricht judgement that it could verify whether the measures adopted by the Union institutions are covered by the contractual authorisation.[35] This case-law was confirmed in the Lisbon judgment.[36] In contrast, the Federal Constitutional Court of Germany limits this position in the Honeywell/Mangold decision to the effect that there must be a sufficiently serious breach of the Union's institutions so that the Federal Constitutional Court can exercise its power.[37] This is the case when the transgression of competencies is evident and leads to a structurally significant shift at the expense of the Member States.[38] Transferred to the measures of the European Central Bank, the European Banking Authority and the Single Resolution Board this means that the drawn authority limits—in Treaties and secondary legislation—are exceeded, if the actors act in the full exercise of its powers in the field of banking supervision and banking regulation. The Federal Constitutional Court of Germany could decide accordingly or refer the matter of the competence basis to the European Court of Justice for a preliminary ruling in accordance to Art 267 TFEU. Both would have come to the conclusion that the European Central Bank and the European agencies are not responsible without a proper legal basis for the adoption of a regulatory administrative act.

The supervisory architecture of the European banking regulation clearly lacks of primarily legislation authorisation. The transfer of sovereign powers to the

[33]Höfling, Gutachten zum 68. Deutschen Juristentag, (C.H. Beck, 2010), F20 et seq.

[34]Sacarcelik, Europäische Bankenunion, Zeitschrift für Bank- und Kapitalmarktrecht (2013), 353 (357).

[35]BVerfGE 89, 155 (186 et seq) paras. 102 et seq. – Maastricht.

[36]BVerfGE 123, 267 – Lissabon.

[37]BVerfGE 126, 286 (304) para. 61, Landau 126, 286 (309) para. 102 – Honeywell/Mangold.

[38]BVerfGE 126, 286 (304) para. 61, Landau 126, 286 (309) para. 102 et seq – Honeywell/Mangold.

European Central Bank, the European Banking Authority or the Single Resolution Board requires changes to the Treaties by the ordinary procedure according to Art 48 (2)–(5) TFEU. In the foreseeable future, such changes to the Treaties are not to be expected in the current political mood.

## 4.2 A Banking Supervision by the European Central Bank Collides with the Target of the Monetary Policy to Maintain Price Stability

The reform of the financial market regulation led to a centralisation of competences at the European Central Bank, which is responsible for the maintenance of price stability and the banking supervisions over the Euro Member States. To understand the dilemma between monetary policy and banking supervision some remarks on the role of the European Central Bank, as well as on the contexts of monetary policy, price stability and banking supervision are necessary. Against this background, the effects of the reforms are discussed.

### *4.2.1 Link Between Monetary Policy and Price Stability*

Already the European treaties take on the relationship between monetary policy and price stability and assign a special role to the European Central Bank. The aims of the European Union require a "for the sustainable development of Europe based on balanced economic growth and price stability" under Art 3 (3) sentence 1 TEU. Art 119 (2) TFEU links the activities of the European Union to "conduct of a single monetary policy and exchange-rate policy the primary objective of both of which shall be to maintain price stability". Systematically consequent commits Art 127 (1) TFEU the European system of central banks to maintain price stability. Rather, Art 128 (1) TFEU justified the sole right of the European Central Bank to determine the supply of banknotes on the market.

The monetary policy of the European Central Bank starts at the central bank money market and includes all measures to control the monetary supply.[39] Through open-market operations the central bank can withdraw or add money to the economic cycle and in this way influence and determine the main refinancing rate (base rate of the European Central Bank).[40] In this way, the price level, i.e. the price

[39]Mankiw and Taylor, Economics, 2nd ed. (South Western Cengage Learning, 2011), 622, 625, 627.

[40]However, the aim is not to influence the interest rate level, but the stability of the price level. The impact of monetary policy decisions on the economy in general and the development of prices in particular are referred to as a transmission mechanism of monetary policy, Europäische Zentralbank, Die Geldpolitik der EZB (2004), 44.

stability is affected.[41] Price stability describes a situation in which neither inflation nor deflation exists.[42] An inflation rate under but close to 2 % is considered as price stability by the European Central Bank. The quantity theory of money explains the relationship between the provided monetary supply and price stability. Formally, the quantity theory can be expressed by the equation $M \cdot V = P \cdot Y$. What lesson can be learned from this relation?

*M* denotes the monetary supply provided by the central bank, which moves with the velocity of circulation (V*)* in the economy. The velocity of circulation refers to the speed at which money changes hands. The right side of equation (*PY*) represents the monetary value of the gross domestic product (*Y*).

What effects of changes in the monetary supply can be derived from the quantity? Empirically, it is easy comprehensible that the velocity *V* is comparatively stable. Accordingly, the rate of change is negligible in time. Thus, a change in the monetary supply on the left side of the equation has a direct impact on the value of the gross domestic product on the right side of the equation. The output of an economy (*Y*) is, however, primarily determined by both the production and the resulting factor on demand, and not by the monetary supply.

A change of *M* is directly reflected in a change in prices. If the central bank increases the monetary supply *M* through open-market operation, the price level (*P*) must also increase in the national economy. The percentage change, in which the price level increases, describes the rate of inflation. The following illustration shows the theoretical relationship between the purchasing power (or the money value), the monetary supply and the price level.

If there is an expansion of the monetary supply, the price level must rise, because the output of the economy has not changed. By implication the value of money falls. The money market is in equilibrium again. The falling course of the monetary demand curve shows that economic actors want to keep more money if the value of money is low in order to acquire goods and services (see Fig. 4.1).

The quantity theory provides the classical context of changes in the monetary supply and the price level. However, if the detailed context over time shall be viewed, impacts in different markets must be analysed in different markets. In the short run an increase in the nominal monetary supply *M,* or rather the real monetary supply *M/P* on the money market,[43] leads to falling interest rates in the economy. Falling interest rates lead to an increase of the economic production in the short run.

---

[41]That means if the Central Bank lowers the main refinancing rate, business banks will expand their lendings, since the necessary liquidity can be gotten cheaper from the Central Bank (first transmission mechanism). The monetary supply in the economy is increasing. This means that the operators also increase their demand for investment loans (second transmission mechanism), Europäische Zentralbank, Die Geldpolitik der EZB (2004), 45.

[42]Europäische Zentralbank, Die Geldpolitik der EZB (2004), 42; for other opinion see Nicolaysen, Rechtsfragen der Währungsunion, (Springer, 1993) 39 et seq. after which price stability is a vague term that cannot be fixed to a specific and quantifiable inflation rate, but must be viewed in the context of the overall economic situation.

[43]With the purchase of securities by the European Central Bank.

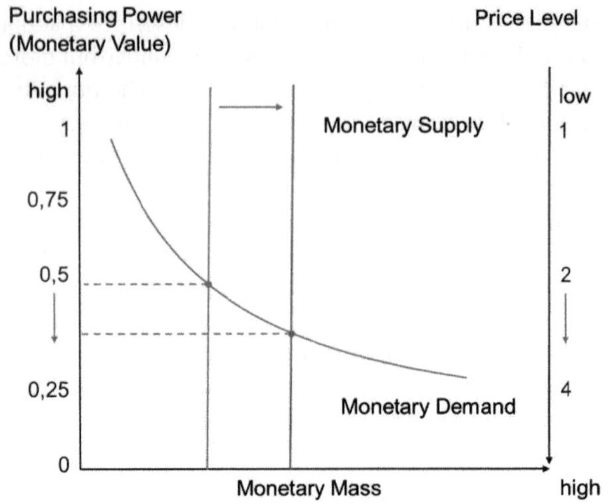


**Fig. 4.1** Relationship between the purchasing power, the monetary supply and the price level (Originally published in Mankiw and Taylor (Eds.), Economics, 2nd ed. 2011, Fig. 30.2, p. 646; used with permission of © Cengage Learning EMEA Ltd. All Rights Reserved.)

In cause of the increased production, unemployment decreases, and wages and prices rise. In the medium term, however, the interest rate rises again because the real monetary supply decreased by the price increase, and the production is declining. Ultimately, monetary policy also leads "only" to an increase of the price level by means of an increased nominal monetary supply. The interest rate and the production in the medium term remain unchanged.[44] The transmission mechanisms fail and the monetary policy can no longer practically maintain price stability.[45]

### *4.2.2 Conflict Between Monetary Policy and Banking Supervision*

The core task of the European Central Bank is to maintain price stability. Due to the reform of the financial regulation law, the European Central Bank has been commissioned by the Single Supervisory Mechanism with banking supervision. Price stability as the primary objective of monetary policy and financial stability as a central objective of banking supervision can compete with each other. In particular, interest rate reductions, loan programmes, the purchase of asset-backed securities or possibly even the purchase of government bonds can lead to the recapitalisation of credit institutes, which are classified to be in risk of default by the banking supervision.

Essential for the supervision by the European Central Bank is the significance of a bank. In accordance with Art 6 (4) second to fifth subparagraph of Regulation (EU)

[44]Blanchard and Johnson, Macroeconomics, 6th ed. (Pearson, 2013) 133 et seq.

[45]Europäische Zentralbank, Die Geldpolitik der EZB (2004), 48.

No 1024/2013 are all banks "significant" that exceed certain thresholds and that significantly act cross-border or receive financial assistance from the European Financial Stability Facility or the European Stability Mechanism, or in any event the three most significant credit institutions in each of the Member States.[46] In addition, of banks considered less significant the European Central Bank can, on Art 6 (5) lit. (b), (d), (e) of Regulation (EU) No 1023/2013, also request information, can after consulting with national competent authorities assume control over the supervision of credit institutions and can decide to exercise directly itself all the relevant powers for one or more credit institutions to ensure consistent application of high supervisory standards. National supervisory authorities remain only with the supervision of credit institutions which fall outside the scope of the Regulation.

The banking supervision by the European Central Bank influences the business behaviour of credit institutions and can lead to failures of monetary policy. Monetary policy failures can lead to an investment trap. An investment trap is when other factors such as the rate of the European Central Bank greatly affect the investment decisions of market participants so that a change of the rate of the European Central Bank has no or only a minor influence on the decisions of economic operators.[47] The money supply is controlled by a reduction or rise in price on refinancing at credit institutions over the base interest rate of the European Central Bank. The first transmission mechanism is the process through which monetary policy decisions of the Central Bank affect the refinancing cost of credit institutions. In addition, the credit institutes have administrative costs which include personnel, material and building costs as well as the costs for supervision. According to Art 51 (1) sentence 1 and 2 of the German Banking Act institutions shall refund to the Federal Government 90 per cent of the costs incurred by Federal Financial Supervisory Authority. The costs shall be apportioned among the individual institutions according to the scale of their business. However, the costs of credit institutions for banking supervision at the Federal Financial Supervisory Authority or the European Central Bank cannot be influenced by the financial institutes.

The result is that credit institutes regularly pass on the cost of banking supervision to businesses and households in determining their rates.[48] Consequently an increase in costs through banking supervision has an effect similar to the increased rate of the European Central Bank. Interest rates increase; thereby investment and consumption plans are less attractive. The result is an investment trap. Thus, the aggregate demand falls again. In the case of an expansionary monetary policy of the

[46]The supervision of the European Central Bank encompasses 120 credit institutions, European Central Bank Press Release 4 September 2014 – Final list of significant credit institutions, (available online, last downloaded 28.02.2015 at: http://www.ecb.europa.eu/press/pr/date/2014/html/pr140904_2.en.html and in particular 21 in Germany: http://www.ecb.europa.eu/pub/pdf/other/ssm-listofsupervisedentities1409en.pdf?59d76de0c5663687f594250ebf228c6b).

[47]Glatzl, Geldpolitik und Bankenaufsicht im Konflikt, (Nomos, 2009), 82 et seq., 194 et seq.

[48]Glatzl, Geldpolitik und Bankenaufsicht im Konflikt, (Nomos, 2009), 197.

European Central Bank and a restrictive banking supervision by the Single Supervisory Mechanism conflicts may be caused. On the one hand, the monetary policy of the European Central Bank leads to an expansion of the volume of money due to the lowered base rates. Thus, the refinancing costs of the credit institutes are reduced. On the other hand, the banking supervisory can also increase the administrative costs of the credit institutes by imposing higher standards in terms of business organisation. An expansionary monetary policy is compensated in full or in part by a restrictive banking supervision.[49] Monetary policy and banking supervision are in a target conflict.

The administrative organisation of the Single Supervisory Mechanism in the European Central Bank is supposed to avoid such failure of monetary policy. Art 19 (1) and (2) of Regulation (EU) No 1024/2013 determines that the banking supervision shall act independently from all bodies of the European Union through the Single Supervisory Mechanism. Art 25 (2) of Regulation No 1024/2013 underlines that the banking supervision to be exercised personally and organisationally separated from monetary policy.[50] This could be followed by the Single Supervisory Mechanism's independence of the European Central Bank. In this sense Art 26 of Regulation (EU) No 1024/2013 establishes an independent supervisory board for decisions of the banking supervision.[51] According to Art 26 (1) of Regulation No 1024/2013, the supervisory board is composed of four representatives of the European Central Bank. Due to the composition of the supervisory board with members of the European Central Bank, the separation within the meaning of Art 25 (2) of Regulation (EU) No 1024/2013 appears rather like a folding screen as the Great Wall of China.[52] The separation may take place within the organisation, but formally the bodies of the European Central Bank direct the banking supervision with their expertise. The European Central Bank cannot be "separated" materially, without creating an entirely new European Union authority. [53] Moreover, under Art 26 (3) of Regulation (EU) No 1024/2013, the Chair and the Vice-Chair are determined by the European Parliament and European Council due to a proposal of the Governing Council of the European Central Bank. The Vice-Chair is again filled by a member of the Executive Board of the European Central Bank. This construction gives less to believe of independence than a mixing of banking supervision and maintenance of price stability. An influence of monetary policy decisions by the Banking supervision cannot be excluded. Furthermore, the supervisory board meets first decisions with reservation; under Art 26 (8) of Regulation (EU) No 1024/2013 they have to be presented to the Council of the

---

[49]Glatzl, Geldpolitik und Bankenaufsicht im Konflikt, (Nomos, 2009), 200.

[50]Underlined by the recitals 65 and 73 of Regulation (EU) 1024/2013.

[51]Art 13 a-o Decision of the European Central Bank of 19 February 2004 adopting the Rules of Procedure of the European Central Bank (ECB/2014/1), OJ L 95, 29.03.2014, p.56.

[52]Kämmerer, Bahn frei der Bankenunion, Neue Zeitschrift für Verwaltungsrecht (2013), 830 (832).

[53]Di Fabio, Die Zukunft einer stabilen Wirtschafts- und Währungsunion: Verfassungs- sowie europarechtliche Grenzen und Möglichkeiten, (Stiftung Familienunternehmen 2013), 60.

European Central Bank. Unless the Council of the European Central Bank does not object, the decision shall be deemed adopted.

However, Art 25 (5) of Regulation (EU) No 1024/2013 opens the possibility to call a mediation panel as arbitration body to resolve differences of views expressed by the competent authorities of participating Member States concerned regarding an objection of the Governing Council to a draft decision by the Supervisory Board. A complete separation of the decisions of the Single Supervisory Mechanism from the Council of the European Central Bank is not possible, since the Council of the European Central Bank is determined as central decision-making body by primary law under Art 129 (1) TFEU and Art (9)–(12) Statute of the European System of Central Banks and the European Central Bank.[54,55]

As a result, there is a dilemma between monetary policy and banking supervision. On the one hand, a concentration of banking supervision and monetary policy at the central bank could lead to synergies. The European Central Bank may—in addition to the national central banks—as "lender of last resort" gain important knowledge about the financial situation of the financial institutions under its supervisions by a continuous supervision.[56] From this, a monetary policy conclusion can be drawn about determination of interest rates for commercial banks refinancing that have an impact on the money supply and the economic price level. On the other hand, a conflict may rise by combining both mandates.[57] There is a risk that the primary orientation of the European Central Bank is softened once reaching the goal of price stability to support the banking sector. In crisis situations that could lead to the situation that the European Central Bank refrains from possible interest rate increases if therewith the financial situation of banks would worsen or the European Central Bank could (as previously announced[58]) acquire toxic balance sheet assets to improve the financial situation of the banks.

---

[54]Protocol (No 4) on the Statute of the European System of Central Banks and of the European Central Bank, OJ C 326, 26.10.2012, p.230.

[55]The same conflict arises between the European Central Banks Governing Council and the European Banking Authorities Board of Supervisors, see Gurlit, The ECB's relationship to EBA, Europäische Zeitschrift für Wirtschaftsrecht (2014), Supplement, 14 (15).

[56]Manger-Nestler and Böttner, Ménage à trois? – Zur gewandelten Rolle der EZB im Spannungsfeld zwischen Geldpolitik, Finanzaufsicht und Fiskalpolitik, Europarecht (2014), 621 (631); Jörgens, Die koordinierte Aufsicht über europaweit tätige Banken (Nomos, 2000), 119, 123.

[57]Sachverständigenrat zur Begutachtung der gesamtwirtschaften Entwicklung, Jahresgutachten 2013/14, (Bonifatius Buch-Druck Verlag, 2013) paras. 253, 255; English version (online available, last downloaded 28.02.2015 at http://www.sachverstaendigenrat-wirtschaft.de/aktuellesjahres gutachten-2013-14.html?&L=1); Manger-Nestler and Böttner, Ménage à trois? – Zur gewandelten Rolle der EZB im Spannungsfeld zwischen Geldpolitik, Finanzaufsicht und Fiskalpolitik, Europarecht (2014), 621 (629 et seq).

[58]European Central Bank Press Release 4 September 2014 – ECB modifies loan-level reporting requirements for some asset-backed securities, (online accessible, last downloaded 28.02.2015 at: http://www.ecb.europa.eu/press/pr/date/2014/html/pr140904_1.en.html).

## 4.3 A National Bank Resolution Due to a European Resolution Fund Leads to a Communitarisation of Liability

The resolution of banks within the meaning of Directive 2014/59/EC aims to prevent a socialisation of risks from bank transactions and losses arising upon their realisation. Therewith, market principles are restored. Investors have to bear the risks resulting from their decision themselves and a "moral hazard" is avoided. This principle is, however, again broken by exceptions provided for by law or the granting of discretion for the Single Resolution Board. The Single Resolution Board is supplemented by a Single Bank Resolution Fund, which replaces the national resolution mechanisms of the participating Member States in accordance with Art 67, 68 of Regulation (EU) No 806/2014. To coordinate the Europeanisation of liability and the Europeanisation of control by the Single Resolution Mechanism at the European Central Bank, there is a gradual transition from an independent, national to a comprehensive financing of resolutions at European level.[59] The process of the unification of Banking at European level is not regulated on the basis of the already weak authority of Art 114 TFEU, but due to an intergovernmental agreement, which sets out the legal basis for the communitarisation of the liability after a ratification by the Member States. The Single Bank Resolution establishes a communitarisation of liability for bank imbalances in the Euro Member States and other participating countries. In particular, a joint liability of banks or States for the costs of a bank resolution can induce a risky economic and financial policy. The benefits of a joint bank resolution occur alone at a national level, while the potential costs are carried by all Member States of the Single Resolution Mechanism. The foundations for a community of solidarity in the sense of a transfer union in Europe were laid tacitly. Adjusting the bank resolution to the banking supervision at a European level sets immense disincentives for a moral hazard of credit institutes and states which have just triggered the previous crisis and have provided the impetus for a comprehensive reform of the financial regulation law.

## 4.4 Banking Supervision Collides with the Model of the Union Law Enforcement

The banking supervision by the European Central Bank in the form of the Single Supervisory Mechanism used national—in Germany the provisions of the Banking Act are used—law while the grant of authority or the withdrawal of authority. It is

[59] Deutsche Bundesbank, Europe's new recovery and resolution regime for credit institutions, 66 Monthly Report, (2014) No.6, 52.

an application of national law by a body of the European Union. Such an administrative enforcement is a novelty that does not fit in the primary law scheme of administrative enforcement in the European Union. Union law is enforced either by institutions of the Union or by Member State authorities. The responsibilities within the enforcement are shared between the Union and the Member States. The administrative enforcement in the European Union is based on rules and exceptions.[60] On the basis of Art 197 (1), 291 (1) TFEU, directly applicable primary law or national implementations of EU legislations of secondary legislations of the European Union are usually enforced by the administration of Member States (indirect enforcement). This form of administrative enforcement also complies with the general principles of conferral Art 5 (2) TEU and subsidiary Art 5 (3) sentence 1 TEU. In contrast, the enforcement of Union law by institutions of the Union (direct enforcement) is the exception, which are anchored in primary legislation of Art 298 (1) TFEU. This penalty can be applied in affairs only concerning the Union—possibly in the European Union budget—or in direct administrative relation with the Member States or individuals.

Under the principle of conferral, Art 5 (2) TEU, the Union shall act only within the limits of the competences. For the legislation Art 3 and 4 TFEU settle regulation of exclusive and shared competences of the European Union. Exclusive competences of the European Union exist within the monetary policy. Banking regulation, hence banking supervision and bank resolution are not subject to monetary policy. According to Art 5 (3) TFEU in areas which do not fall within its exclusive competence, the Union shall act only if and in so far as the objectives of the proposed action cannot be sufficiently achieved by the Member States, either at central level or at regional and local level, but can rather, by reason of the scale or effects of the proposed action, be better achieved at Union level. As a result, the European Union cannot claim any administrative competencies without corresponding legislative powers.[61] The Banking Supervision of the European Central Bank is not compatible with the Union law principle of subsidiarity.

Such a strict dichotomous separation, however, is difficult to obtain during times of pluralisation and diversification of administrative actions. Increasing obligations to inform, assist and coordinate as well as consultation and participation rights lead to complex interdependence of national administrations during the administrative enforcement. The European Composite Administration developed.[62] Guiding

[60]Rengeling, Rechtsgrundsätze beim Verwaltungsvollzug des Europäischen Gemeinschaftsrechts, (Carl Heymanns Verlag, 1977) 9 et seq.; S. Augsberg, Europäisches Verwaltungsorganisationsrecht und Vollzugsformen, in Terhechte (Ed.), Verwaltungsrecht der EU, (Nomos, 2010), § 6 paras. 14 et seq.

[61]Bast, in Grabitz, Hilf and Nettesheim (Eds.), EUV/AEUV Commentary, 53rd ed. (C.H. Beck 2014), Art 5 TEU, para. 53.

[62]Schmidt-Aßmann, Einleitung: Der Europäische Verwaltungsverbund und die Rolle des Europäischen Verwaltungsrechts, in Schmidt-Aßmann and Schöndorf-Haubold (Eds.), Der Europäische Verwaltungsverbund, (Mohr Siebeck, 2005) 1 et seq.; Weiß, Der Europäische Verwaltungsverbund, (Duncker & Humblot, 2010).

principle of this Composite Administration is a coherent enforcement of European Union law, whereby the strict separation of indirect and direct enforcement is softened.[63] The Banking Supervision of the European Central Bank through the Single Supervisory Mechanism breaks the rule of indirect Member State enforcement and represents a direct enforcement by the Union. Special quality is that the European Central Bank enforces no substantive European Union law, but national law.[64] The reason for this lies in the fragmentation of the substantive Banking Supervision Law in the Member States whose currency is the euro. There are a large number of different codifications in directives and regulations, but a unified Regulatory Law through technical regulatory and implementing standards and a single rule book of the European Banking Authority do not yet exist. Due to a lack of uniform European rules no consistent enforcement of European Union law takes place, but instead an individual enforcement of national law is taking place. A possible different application and interpretation of national provisions at national and European level could lead to a fragmentation of banking supervision.[65] That would be exactly the opposite of a coherent administrative enforcement, which is the aim of the European Composite Administration. As result, constitutionally problems of judicial protection would emerge. The application of national rules by the European Central Bank is not compatible with the constitutional requirement of effective legal protection of Art 19 (4) of the German Basic Law. First, in the context of actions for annulment or for failure and the preliminary ruling procedure, Union courts are responsible for the control of the actions of institutions of the Union. However, the European Central Bank as an institution of the European Union only applies national rules pursuant to Art 13 (1) TEU. The application and interpretation of national provisions by Union institutions are not checked by Union courts.[66] Effective legal protection by national courts is also ruled out. Union institutions are not subject to German jurisdiction.[67] As a result, no judicial review of the enforcement of national rules by Unions institutions is possible. Countermeasures of the European Central Bank through banking supervision are no effective legal protection within the meaning of Art 19 (4) of German Basic Law. The banking supervision by the European Central Bank is not compatible with the principle of subsidiarity of Art 5 (3) TEU nor with the national rule of law and its principle of effective legal protection.

---

[63]Peuker, Die Anwendung nationaler Rechtsvorschriften durch Unionsorgane – ein Konstruktionsfehler der europäischen Bankenaufsicht, Juristische Zeitung (2014), 764 (765 et seq.).

[64]Neumann, The supervisory powers of national authorities and cooperation with the ECB - a new epoch a banking supervision, Europäische Zeitschrift für Wirtschaftsrecht (2014), Supplement, 9 (13).

[65]Sacarcelik, Europäische Bankenunion, Zeitschrift für Bank- und Kapitalmarktrecht (2013), 353 (358).

[66]Schneider, Inconsistencies and unsolved Problems in the European Banking Union, Europäische Zeitschrift für Wirtschaftsrecht (2013), 452 (456).

[67]BVerfGE 58, 1.

## 4.5 Democratically the Banking Regulation Is Only Poorly Legitimised

Democratically banking regulation in the European Union is only poorly legitimised in terms of European and German standards. An independent banking supervision by the European Central Bank, a banking regulation by the European Banking Authority and a bank resolution by the Single Supervisory Mechanism constitute a far-reaching transfer of sovereignty to the European level, which generally requires a direct, democratic legitimacy.

### *4.5.1 Principle of Democratic Legitimisation*

In the context of pluralism and Europeanisation of the administrative organisation constitutional problems are created, since the administrative organisation requires democratic legitimacy.[68]

Democratic legitimacy requires a more immediate relationship of accountability between the people through the elected parliament to the appointed executive of the person in office.[69] This is the core idea of an unbroken chain of legitimacy. In addition, the administration is bound to the people and their representatives.[70] This binding is reflected in the bond of administration to law and the responsibility of the administration to the Parliament as a representative of the people.[71]

At first glance, the legitimacy of an independent regulatory body such as the European Central Bank seems difficult to reconcile with the requirement of an unbroken chain of legitimacy from the people to the relevant administrative body

[68]Trute, Die Verwaltung und das Verwaltungsrecht zwischen gesellschaftlicher Selbstregulierung und staatlicher Steuerung, Deutsches Verwaltungsblatt (1996), 950 (963); Trute, Verantwortungsteilung als Schlüsselbegriff eines sich verändernden Verhältnisses von öffentlichem und privatem Sektor, in Schuppert (Ed.), Jenseits von Privatisierung und "schlankem" Staat, (Nomos, 1999), 13 (31 et seq.); confirmed especially for regulatory authorities in Europe, by Shapiro, The problems of independant agencies in the United States and the European Union, 4 Journal of European Public Policy (1997), 276 (283 et seq.).

[69]Critical but differentiated Ludwigs, Die Bundesnetzagentur auf dem Weg zur independant agency? – Europarechtliche Anstöße und verfassungsrechtliche Grenzen, Die Verwaltung (2010), 41 (45 et seq.); Gärditz, Europäisches Regulierungsverwaltungsrecht auf Abwegen, 135 Archiv des öffentlichen Rechts (2010), 251 (277, 284 et seq.) Regards already the political independence of an independent authority as exception requiring legitimisation and considers this exception in the provision of broad scopes for decision-making for the regulating market design as incompatible with the principle of democracy.

[70]Böckenförde, Demokratie als Verfassungsprinzip, in Isensee and Kirchhof (Eds.), Handbuch des Staatsrechts – Vol.II, 3rd ed. (C.F. Müller, 2004) § 24 paras.21 et seq.

[71]Trute, Die demokratische Legitimation der Verwaltung, in Hoffmann-Riem, Schmidt-Aßmann and Voßkuhle (Eds.), Grundlagen des Verwaltungsrechts – Vol.1, 2nd ed. (C.H. Beck, 2012), § 6 paras.11 et seq.

and its decision. But an unbroken chain of legitimacy is not a rigid framework.[72] Since the legitimacy of banking regulation and its decisions is put down to the people, the neutrality and objectivity of administration of particular interests is guaranteed at the various stages of the chain of legitimacy. According to Art 20 (2) sentence 1 German Basic Law the idea behind this is that all State power emanates from the people. Moreover, Art 20 (2) German Basic Law does not prescribe any particular legitimacy requirements. A certain level of democratic legitimacy is sufficient, provided that the required effectiveness democratic legitimacy of Art 20 (2) German Basic Law is ensured.[73] Not the form, but the effectiveness of democratic legitimacy is crucial. Thus, instead of a direct chain of legitimacy also an appropriate level of legitimacy through the interaction of different forms of legitimacy within the meaning of the principle of democracy is sufficient.[74]

### *4.5.2 Democratic Legitimacy of Independent Regulatory Actors*

The banking supervision by the European Central Bank is carried out in an independent manner according to Art 130 TFEU and is in a state of tension to the principle of democracy, which is part of the basic values of the European Union pursuant to Art 2 sentence 1 TEU. According to Art 10 (1) TEU the functioning of the Union shall be founded on representative democracy. This means that any form of independent exercise of sovereign authority under the liberation of political control by the European Parliament, the Council or the Commission requires a justification. Such a justification is also required by the German constitutional law in Art 23 (1) sentence 2 German Basic Law by adopting an approval law for any transfer of sovereignty. Any non-conforming to the democratic principle by the transfer of sovereign powers to independent institutions of the European Union requires a justification by a high-level concern.[75]

The connection of the monetary policy to the independence of the central bank could be such a high-level concern. Politically and economically it corresponds with the sense and purpose of the currency system to establish an independent

---

[72]Böckenförde, Demokratie als Verfassungsprinzip, in Isensee and Kirchhof (Eds.), Handbuch des Staatsrechts – Vol.II, 3rd ed. (C.F. Müller, 2004) § 24 para.23.

[73]Böckenförde, Demokratie als Verfassungsprinzip, in Isensee and Kirchhof (Eds.), Handbuch des Staatsrechts – Vol.II, 3rd ed. (C.F. Müller, 2004) § 24 para.23.

[74]BVerfGE 83, 37 (50 f.), 60 (72); Trute, Die demokratische Legitimation der Verwaltung, in Hoffmann-Riem, Schmidt-Aßmann and Voßkuhle (Eds.), Grundlagen des Verwaltungsrechts – Vol.1, 2nd ed. (C.H. Beck, 2012), § 6 para. 14; Herdegen, in Maunz/Dürig, Grundgesetz. Kommentar, Stand: 69. Lfg. Mai 2013, Art 79 Rdnr.128; Jestaedt, Demokratieprinzip und Kondominialverwaltung, Berlin 1993, 285 et seq.; 288 et seq., 297 et seq.

[75]See a general discussion of this problem in Wolfers and Voland, Europäische Zentralbank und Bankenaufsicht, Zeitschrift für Bank- und Kapitalmarktrecht (2014), 177 (183 et seq).

central bank, which is not subjected to any national or supranational responsibility, to withdraw the monetary policy from an access by interest groups.[76] Therefore, the European Central Bank shall not seek or take instructions from Union institutions, bodies, offices or agencies, from any government of a Member State or from any other body as defined in Art 139 TFEU. This limitation of the democratic legitimacy, coming from the voters in the Member States, was transferred to Art 88 sentence 2 German Law in the German constitutional law. This is a limitation of the guarantee in perpetuity of Article 79 (3) German Basic Law, which declared, among other things, a change of principles laid down in Art 20 German Basic Law—as the principle of democracy in accordance with Art 20 (1) sentence 1 German Basic Law—inadmissible. Such a modification of the democratic principle according to Art 88 sentence 2 German Basic Law is compatible with Art 79 (3) German Basic Law, as long as the will of the constitution-amending legislature seems to aim for a constitutional basis for the monetary union as planned within the Treaty on European Union.[77] Already in the Maastricht Treaty, the Federal Constitutional Court of Germany declared that the creation of independent authorities, linked with this matter, shall be limited to this matter.[78] It follows that the creation of the European Central Bank as an independent institution serves solely for monetary policy and price stability. A far-reaching independence, for example, for banking supervision is not provided. In addition, the connection of monetary policy with an independent central bank is a high-level concern, which can be verified empirically.[79] Such an empirical connection is missing between the banking supervision and the stability of the financial system.[80]

It is questionable whether such a banking supervision by the European Central Bank can be democratically legitimised. Basically, the members of the Council of the European Central Bank are democratically legitimated by the respective personnel of the sending Member States. Furthermore, they are not parliamentary responsible within the exercise of its powers in terms of the transferred set of tasks, in accordance with Art 282 (3) TFEU. In the European or German law, such a high degree of independence can only be compared with the independence of the judiciary, Art 253 (1) TFEU; Art 97 (1) German Basic Law. In general, with the contractual or constitutional granting of independence, certain parts of the public authority are taken away from the immediate access of the parliamentary control in order to provide control forces and counterweights to democratic majority decisions.[81] The Parliament restricts itself, and it has forgone its democratically

[76]BVerfGE 89, 155 (169 et seq) para 152 – Maastricht.

[77]BVerfGE 89, 155 (208) para. 152 – Maastricht.

[78]BVerfGE 89, 155 (208) para. 152 – Maastricht.

[79]BVerfGE 89, 155 (208 et seq.) – Maastricht.

[80]Herdegen, Europäische Bankenunion, Wertpapiermitteilungen (2012), 1889 (1894).

[81]Di Fabio, Die Zukunft einer stabilen Wirtschafts- und Währungsunion: Verfassungs- sowie europarechtliche Grenzen und Möglichkeiten, (Stiftung Familienunternehmen, 2013), 41.

legitimised responsibility.[82] Rather the redemption of control can constitute a particular form of exercising this democratically legitimised responsibility.[83] It is an element of the constitutional principle of separation of powers, which complements the principle of democracy, in order to limit mistakes of political leadership.[84] Just as judges are bound by law (Art 19 (1) TEU, Art 20 (3) German Basic Law), the European Central Bank is bound to the needs of a stable currency, tied with the explicit aim of price stability, Art 127 (1) sentence 1 and Art 282 (2) sentence 1 TFEU. Conversely, all measures of the European Central Bank outside the monetary policy—such as banking supervision—are not covered by the respective competence requirements. It follows that with the acquisition of banking supervision by the European Central Bank especially the contractual justification for its independence and, at the same time, the exception of direct democratic legitimacy.[85] The supervision of banks is the basis for a potential resolution of banks, which could lead to a far-reaching intervention in national economies and private enterprises, must be reasoned parliamentary.[86] The banking supervision by the European Central Bank and the subsequent possible bank resolution by the Single Resolution Board is insufficiently democratically legitimised.

### *4.5.3 Fundamental Weaknesses of the Democratic Legitimacy of Decisions of Independent Regulatory Actors*

It is crucial that a democratic legitimacy according to Art 10 TFEU is ensured that also takes the demographic conditions into account. In particular, the involvement of national central banks in the Council of the European Central Bank—in matters that exceed the monetary policy—or national supervisory authorities in the Council of the European Banking Authority both collide with the principle of representative democracy.[87] By formally balanced participation of national representatives in the respective bodies (Council of the European Central Bank, Board of Supervisors of the European Banking Authority, Supervisory Board of the Single Supervisory

---

[82]Häde, Jenseits der Effizienz: Wer kontrolliert die Kontrolleure? Europäische Zeitschrift für Wirtschaftsrecht (2011), 662 (664).

[83]Ruffert, Verselbständigte Verwaltungseinheiten: Ein europäischer Megatrend im Vergleich, in Trute, Groß, Röhl and Möllers (Eds.), Allgemeines Verwaltungsrecht – zur Tragfähigkeit eines Konzepts, (Mohr Siebeck, 2008), 431 (454).

[84]Di Fabio, Die Zukunft einer stabilen Wirtschafts- und Währungsunion: Verfassungs- sowie europarechtliche Grenzen und Möglichkeiten, (Stiftung Familienunternehmen, 2013), 41 et seq.

[85]Di Fabio, Die Zukunft einer stabilen Wirtschafts- und Währungsunion: Verfassungs- sowie europarechtliche Grenzen und Möglichkeiten, (Stiftung Familienunternehmen, 2013), 43.

[86]Di Fabio, Die Zukunft einer stabilen Wirtschafts- und Währungsunion: Verfassungs- sowie europarechtliche Grenzen und Möglichkeiten, (Stiftung Familienunternehmen, 2013), 57 et seq.

[87]Herdegen, Europäische Bankenunion, Wertpapiermitteilungen (2012), 1889 (1896).

Mechanism) there is a danger that a majority of representatives of less populous, particularly crisis-prone or economically distressed Member States decide in favour of a casual exercise of banking supervision, of the purchase of credit securitisations or government bonds, for the development of further regulatory and implementing standards or for the waiver of a more appropriate resolution by a simple majority for.[88] The principles of representative democracy are shaken due to the concentration of executive decision-making powers in a regulatory central area, more precisely, in facilities such as the Single Resolution Board or the Board of Supervisors of the European Banking Authority and even more significantly at the European Central Bank, which are filled according to the principle of equality of states and not by population size or risk of liability.[89]

In this sense, it is particularly disappointing that each President of the participating central banks in the Council of the European Central Bank shall have one vote each according to the principle of formal equality. As of 01.01.2015 the voting rights in the Council of the European Central Bank are subject to a rota system. With the accession of Lithuania to the euro area more than 18 governors will be represented in the Council of the European Central Bank for the first time.[90] Therewith, a new voting procedure is put into force. At meetings of the Council of the European Central Bank, the votes of all members are heard and counted. In addition to six members of the Executive Board of the European Central Bank, this currently includes 18 presidents and governors of the national central banks of the Euro system. According to the rota systems, the Governors are divided into groups according to the size of their economies and their financial sectors.[91] The largest five countries form the first group. They share four voting rights. This group includes Germany, France, Italy, Spain and the Netherlands. The voices within this group rotate on a monthly basis, so that each month one of the Governors of the five largest countries has no vote in the Council.[92] In other words, every five months the President of the Deutsche Bundesbank loses the right to vote on decisions in the Council of the European Central Bank, which represents a serious breach of the principle of democracy in terms of a representation of national interests of the peoples of the Member States.

[88]Herdegen, Europäische Bankenunion, Wertpapiermitteilungen (2012), 1889 (1896).

[89]Di Fabio, Die Zukunft einer stabilen Wirtschafts- und Währungsunion: Verfassungs- sowie europarechtliche Grenzen und Möglichkeiten, (Stiftung Familienunternehmen, 2013), 60.

[90]Art 10.1 of the Statute of the European System of Central Banks and the European Central Bank.

[91]Art 10.2 of the Statute of the European System of Central Banks and of the European Central Bank in conjunction with Art 3a Decision of the European Central Bank of 19 February 2004 adopting the Rules of Procedure of the European Central Bank (ECB/2014/1), OJ L 95, 29.03.2014, p.56.

[92]Art 3a (3) and (4) Decision of the European Central Bank of 19 February 2004 adopting the Rules of Procedure of the European Central Bank (ECB/2014/1).

## 4.6 The Regulatory Density of the Institutional Framework of Regulatory Actors Influences the Organisational Power of the Regulatory Actors

The classification of the actors of banking regulation in model types allows a systematisation of administrative organisations according to their influence on decisions. The influence on regulatory decisions especially depends on the bodies of the organisation. The more comprehensive the regulatory framework is regulated by law, regulation or statute, the more differentiated are institutional arrangements that determine the particular competencies and information relations of the organisation. From this, an organisation chain can be derived based on the respective influence of the organisation on regulatory decisions and allocate the appropriate actors (see Fig. 4.2).

The development of the regulatory framework is carried out at international level by the Financial Stability Board and the Basel Committee on Banking Supervision, whose legal bases are broad statutes under international law. As committees of large economies and financial traders, they serve the exchange of experience and information and give globally recognised impulses for regulations. The Federal Republic of Germany participates by the Federal Ministry of Finance and the Deutsche Bundesbank.

Impulses at international level are taken at European level by the European Commission and the European Banking Authority and are processed on the basis of their institutional arrangements. The control density results from the European Treaties for the European Commission and Regulation (EU) No 1093/2010 establishing the European Banking Authority—they provide decision-making structures and procedures. Thus, the impulses are either processed to proposals for directives and regulations by the European Commission or to technical regulatory and implementing standards by the European Banking Authority at international

**Fig. 4.2** Types of administrative organisation in the field of banking regulation

level. This process includes both the Federal Ministry of Finance at the European Commission and the Federal Financial Supervisory Authority, as well as the Deutsche Bundesbank at the European Banking Authority as representatives of the German interests. The proposals for directives and regulations of the European Commission become legally binding regulatory programmes with the help of the European Parliament and the Council in accordance with their contractually defined roles in the ordinary legislative procedure. These regulatory programs prepare the framework for the regulatory decisions of the European Central Bank as well as the national supervisory and resolution authorities. In contrast, the European Commission decides on the drafts of technical regulatory and implementing standards, which thereby are directly applicable in the Member States. These regulatory programmes are carried out in the area of banking supervision by the European Central Bank in the form of the Single Supervisory Mechanism and the Federal Financial Supervisory Authority, whereas the Single Resolution Board and the Federal Agency for Financial Market Stabilisation are responsible for in the area of resolution. Legal basis of these actors are regulations of the European Union, in particular the Banking Act, which determine the powers and procedures of supervisory and resolution committees. The supervision of the implementation of regulatory decisions, the monitoring of credit institutions and the supervision of financial markets take place at an international level by the International Monetary Fund and the Basel Committee on Banking Supervision, which can detect violations in a politically effective way, and may also sanction these violation at European level by the European Central Bank and the European Banking Authority.

This organisation chain allows a systematisation of administrative organisations in the process of banking regulation in Germany and Europe.

## 4.7 Organisational Powers Correlate with the Influence of Regulatory Actors on Decisions

To answer the research question, the actors of banking regulation can be classified in a matrix between organisational power and their influence on the decision-making (see Fig. 4.3). Scale for the determination of organisational power are again the institutional arrangements that determine via the principles of organisation the decision-making and the governing bodies. The greater the institutional organisational power is, the more competencies decision-making bodies get. The organisational power increases over four steps from low to high. Groups and committees are Forums that have low organisational power. In contrast, the national central banks as expert groups have a higher organisational power. European institutions and European agencies are governing bodies. The highest organisational power is given to independent, judicial-like committees at European and national level. In contrast, the influence on decisions also rises on four stages from low to high. It is

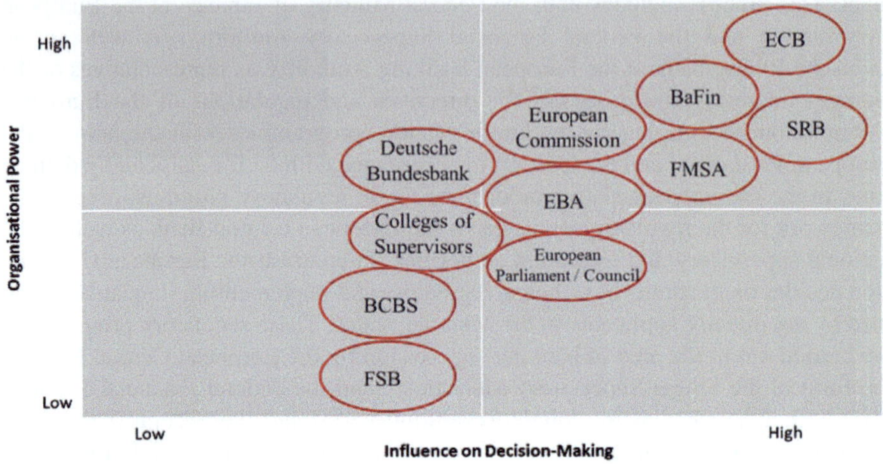


**Fig. 4.3** Matrix of organisational power and influence on decision-making

distinguished from a non-binding right to contribute, to a binding right to include up to programming and final decisions.

The Financial Stability Board (FSB) and the Basel Committee on Banking Supervision (BCBS) are international bodies that consist of governments, central banks, supervisory authorities and credit institutes. These are open forums, which are open for new members to vote for a framework for the regulation of global financial markets at international level. There is no relationship of superiority or inferiority between the members. These forums focus on the exchange of experiences and information. They have no binding participation and decision competence. Even the most widely used standards are legally not binding; they serve only as recommendation as they are a soft law of international law, merely a recommendation.[93] Nevertheless, the Financial Stability Board and the Basel Committee on Banking Supervision have factual a considerable influence on decisions, since they represent the main actors of developed and emerging countries, whose decisions and recommendations have a politically and morally self-binding effect for the development of guidelines and standards for the regulation of the financial market.

Expert bodies and the national central banks have a higher organisational power, which have to be included in regulations at the European level. The Deutsche Bundesbank takes over the ongoing supervision of credit institutes and prepares with their administrative structures the decisions of the Federal Financial Supervisory Authority. The central areas and departments make decisions on the basis of the German Federal Bank Act according to the traditional administrative hierarchy. Through the participation and cooperation of the Deutsche Bundesbank in the

[93]Giovanoli, Reflections on International Financial Standards as ‘Soft Law’, 37 Essays in International Financial and Economic Law (2002), 1(8).

Financial Stability Board, the Basel Committee on Banking Supervision and the European Banking Authority (EBA) various opportunities to influence decisions are given, but a binding decision-making power for the banking regulation is missing.

Governing bodies have an even greater influence on decisions at European level. The European Commission can influence the European Parliaments and Councils programming of rules for the regulation of financial markets and institutions both by drafting regulations and directives and by deciding on technical regulatory and implementing standards, which in turn are developed by the European Banking Authority.

National authorities and independent judicial-like committees have the largest organisational power at European level. The Federal Financial Supervisory Authority (BaFin) makes immediate supervisory decisions and the Federal Agency for Financial Market Stabilisation (FMSA) makes binding recovery or resolution decisions according to the hierarchy of their departments and units, if and to the extent that European institutions of Single Supervisory Mechanism and the Single Resolution Board (SRB) are not responsible and do not intervene in individual cases. In contrast, through the judicial-like independence of the Council of the European Central Bank and its influence on the Supervisory Board, the European Central Bank (ECB) has the greatest influence on regulatory decisions towards individual credit institutes.

# Chapter 5
# Summary

The study of the organisation of banking regulation was under the general question "does organisation matter?" which can be answered clearly: organisation matters! Administrative organisation is composed of certain elements that affect the administrative action of an administrative unit. Particularly, institutional arrangements build a basis for the design of organisational units. They rather create organisational relationships between banking regulation actors in a multi-level system, whereby information is exchanged, regulatory uncertainties are overcome and decisions are made uniformly.

Furthermore, there are correlations between institutional arrangements and, in particular, the legal form, the decision form, competencies and organisational relationships of administrative organisations. Therewith, actors of banking regulation can be classified into five model types. The model types fit into a range that extends from the development, to the decision and to the control of regulatory measures.

The system of banking regulation at European level in cooperation with the international and European level lacks comprehensive and undisputed legal bases for the establishment of a variety of banking regulators. In particular, the central role of the European Central Bank within the system of banking supervision and its impact on banking regulation and bank resolution is in conflict with the maintenance of price stability.

Basic constitutional tensions could be eliminated by taking into account its demographics or its respective financial strength. However, such a provision in the Statute of the European System of Central Banks and the European Central Bank does not seem politically feasible. At the same time, graded voting rights, in favour of larger Member States, do not lead to an increased appropriateness.[1]

The banking supervision law was unified under the Capital Requirements Directive IV and the Capital Requirements Regulation. This materially unification is accompanied by a formal centralisation of structures. As from November 2014,

[1]Herdegen, Europäische Bankenunion, Wertpapiermitteilungen (2012), 1889 (1896).



A. Wellerdt, *Organisation of Banking Regulation*, SpringerBriefs in Law,
DOI 10.1007/978-3-319-17638-3_5

a double-tracked banking supervision of credit institutions has been established, which is perceived—according to the importance of the banks for the financial system by the European Central Bank—in form of the Single Supervisory Mechanism or the Federal Financial Supervisory Authority. This increases the complexity of the European supervision because it poses greater demands on the exchange of information and the consistency of supervisory measures, which again increases the error rate. A centralisation of supervision can only be successful if the supervision orients itself on high standards and not on the lowest common denominator. In this case egalitarianism can be a systemic risk itself. A competition of the supervisory system would be ideal in a given international framework within the meaning of the greatest common multiple of the supervisory levels.

In the area of banking supervision a union-wide standardisation of the substantive law takes place due to the Banking Recovery and Resolution Directive. Therewith, specially tailored resolution rules were created to avoid the shortcomings of general insolvency law and consequential "bail-outs" of banks. In contrast to banking supervision, bank resolution was not formally centralised, but left to the authorities of the Member States.

Overall, a fragmentation of the European regulatory regime is carried out by the Single Supervisory Mechanism and the Single Resolution Mechanism. The new supervisory architecture for financial institutions only extends to those, whose place of business is in a Member State whose currency is the euro. Conversely, the contractual freedom of establishment[2] gives a credit institute the right to place his business outside the scope of the European Central Bank. Again this results in a danger to avoid regulation, or at least to delay a uniform regulation in the European Union. The Single Resolution Mechanism theoretically applies in all Member States of the European Union, but in fact only those States are recognised that participate in the Single Supervisory Mechanism.

The particular question in which manner organisations influence the decision-making process in banking regulation may be answered in principle with the help of model types according to their respective contribution in the development, processing, preparation, execution and control. At the same time, a centralisation of banking regulation is made clear at European level that more and more withdraws the regulation of financial markets from the influence of the Member States.

[2]In Interpretation of ECJ, Decision of 05.11.2002, C-208/00 Überseering BV/Nordic Construction Company [2002], ECR I-9919 = Europäische Zeitschrift für Wirtschaftsrecht (2002), 754.

# References


*Albers, Marion,* Umgang mit personenbezogenen Informationen und Daten, in Hoffmann-Riem, Wolfgang, Schmidt-Aßmann, Eberhard and Voßkuhle, Andreas (Eds.), Grundlagen des Verwaltungsrechts – Volume 2: Informationsordnung, Verwaltungsverfahren, Handlungsformen, 2nd ed. (München: C. H. Beck, 2012), § 22.

*Appel, Ivo,* Methodik des Umgangs mit Ungewissheit, in Schmidt-Aßmann, Eberhard and Hoffmann-Riem, Wolfgang (Eds.), Methoden der Verwaltungswissenschaft, (Nomos: Baden-Baden, 2004), pp. 329–336.

*Arrow, Kenneth J.*, Essays in the theory of risk-bearing, (Amsterdam: North-Holland Publications, 1971).

*Augsberg, Ino*, Selbstreferenz als Gesetzgebungsprogramm, Kritische Vierteljahresschrift für Gesetzgebung und Rechtswissenschaft, 2007, pp. 236–255.

*Augsberg, Steffen,* Europäisches Verwaltungsorganisationsrecht und Vollzugsformen, in Terhechte, Jörg Philipp (Ed.), Verwaltungsrecht der EU, (Baden-Baden: Nomos, 2010), § 6.

*Augsberg,* Steffen, Der Staat als Informationsmittler, Deutsches Verwaltungsblatt, 2007, pp. 733–741.

*Augsberg,* Steffen, Rechtsetzung zwischen Staat und Gesellschaft, (Berlin: Duncker & Humblot, 2003).

*Baldwin, Robert, Cave Martin and Lodge, Martin* (Eds.), Understanding Regulation: theory, strategy and practice, 2nd ed. (Oxford: Oxford University Press, 2012).

*Bang, Henrik P.*, Introduction, in Bang, Henrik P. (Ed.), Governance as social and political communication, (Manchester: Manchester University Press, 2003).

*Benz, Angelika and König, Klaus*, Privatisierung und staatliche Regulierung – eine Zwischenbilanz, in Benz, Angelika and König, Klaus (Eds.), Privatisierung und staatliche Regulierung, (Baden-Baden: Nomos, 1997).

*Benz, Arthur*, Einleitung: Governance – Modebegriff oder nützliches sozialwissenschaftliches Konzept?, in Benz, Arthur (Ed.), Governance – Regieren in komplexen Regelsystemen. Einführung, 2nd ed. (Wiesbaden: VS Verlag für Sozialwissenschaften, 2012).

*Benz, Arthur*, Der moderne Staat – Grundlagen der politologischen Analyse, 2nd ed. (München: Oldenbourg, 2009).

*Berringer, Christian*, Regulierung als Erscheinungsform der Wirtschaftsaufsicht, (München: C.H. Beck, 2004).

*Bieg, Harmut, Krämer, Gregor and Waschbusch, Gerd*, Bankenaufsicht in Theorie und Praxis, 3rd ed. (Frankfurt am Main: Frankfurt School Verlag, 2009).

*Blanchard, Olivier and Johnson, David*, Macroeconomics, 6th ed. (Boston: Pearson, 2013).

*Brohm, Winfried*, Strukturen der Wirtschaftsverwaltung, (Stuttgart: Kohlhammer, 1969).

*Böckenförde, Wolfgang*, Demokratie als Verfassungsprinzip, in Isensee, Josef and Kirchhof, Paul (Eds.), Handbuch des Staatsrechts – Volume II: Verfassungsstaat, 3rd ed. (Heidelberg: C. F. Müller, 2004).




A. Wellerdt, *Organisation of Banking Regulation*, SpringerBriefs in Law,
DOI 10.1007/978-3-319-17638-3

*Bofinger, Peter*, Grundzüge der Volkswirtschaftslehre. Eine Einführung in die Wissenschaft von Märkten, 3rd ed. (München: Pearson Studium, 2011).

*Bormann, Jörg and Finsinger, Jörg*, Markt und Regulierung, (München: Vahlen, 1999).

*Boos, Karl-Heinz, Fischer, Reinfrid and Schulte-Mattler, Hermann* (Eds.), Kreditwesengesetz, Kommentar, 4th ed. (München: C. H. Beck, 2012).

*Bumke, Christian*, Kapitalmarktregulierung – Eine Untersuchung über Konzeption und Dogmatik des Regulierungsverwaltungsrechts, Die Verwaltung (2008), pp. 227–257.

*Burgi, Martin*, Verwaltungsorganisationsrecht, in Erichsen, Hans-Uwe and Ehlers, Dirk (Eds.), Allgemeines Verwaltungsrecht, 14th ed. (Berlin/New York: De Gruyter, 2010), § 7.

*Bull, Hans Peter and Mehde, Veith*, Allgemeines Verwaltungsrecht, 8th ed. (Heidelberg: C. F. Müller, 2009).

*Calliess, Christian and Ruffert, Matthias* (Eds.), EUV/AEUV Kommentar, Das Verfassungsrecht der Europäischen Union mit Grundrechtecharta, 4th ed. (München: C.H. Beck, 2011).

*Coase, Ronald*, The problem of social cost, Journal of Law and Economics, 1960, pp. 1–44.

*Ceyssens, Jan*, Teufelskreis zwischen Banken und Staatsfinanzen – Der Europäische Bankaufsichtsmechanimus, Neue Juristische Wochenschrift (2013), pp. 3704–3708.

*Deutsche Bundesbank*, Europe's new recovery and resolution regime for credit institutions, 66 Monthly Report No.6 (2014), pp. 31–57.

*Deutsche Bundesbank*, European Single Supervisory Mechanism for banks – a first step on the road to a banking union, 65 Monthly Report, No.7 (2013), pp. 13–34.

*Deutsche Bundesbank*, Macroprudential Oversight in Germany: framework, institutions and tools, 65 Monthly Report No.4 (2013), pp. 39–54.

*Deutsche Bundesbank*, International cooperation in banking regulation: past and present, 63 Monthly Report No.9 (2011), pp. 79–93.

*Deutsche Bundesbank*, Basel III – Leitfaden zu den neuen Eigenkapital und Liquiditätsregeln für Banken, Bundesbankpublikation (Frankfurt am Main: Deutsche Bundesbank, 2011).

*Di Fabio, Udo*, Die Zukunft einer stabilen Wirtschafts- und Währungsunion – Verfassungs- sowie europarechtliche Grenzen und Möglichkeiten, (München: Stiftung Familienunternehmen, 2013).

*Ehlers, Dirk*, Staatliche Verwaltung, in Erichsen, Hans-Uwe and Ehlers, Dirk (Eds.), Allgemeines Verwaltungsrecht, 14th ed. (Berlin/New York: de Gruyter, 2010), § 1.

*Eichenberger, Reiner*, Wissen und Information in ökonomischer Perspektive, in Engel, Christoph, Halfmann, Jost and Schulte, Martin (Eds.), Wissen – Nichtwissen – Unsicheres Wissen, (Baden-Baden: Nomos, 2002), pp. 76–92.

*Eifert, Martin*, Regulierungsstrategien, in Hoffmann-Riem, Wolfgang, Schmidt-Aßmann, Eberhard and Voßkuhle, Andreas (Eds.), Grundlagen des Verwaltungsrechts – Volume 1: Methoden, Maßstäbe, Aufgaben, Organisation, 2nd ed. (München: C. H. Beck, 2012), § 19.

*Eifert, Martin*, Innovation in und durch Netzwerkorganisation: Relevanz, Regulierung und staatliche Einbindung, in Eifert, Martin and Hoffmann-Riem, Wolfgang (Eds.), Innovation und rechtliche Regulierung, (Baden-Baden: Nomos, 2002).

*Ellwein, Thomas*, Regieren und Verwalten – Eine kritische Einführung, (Opladen: Westdeutscher Verlag, 1976).

*Ellwein, Thomas*, Einführung in die Regierungs- und Verwaltungslehre, (Stuttgart: Kohlhammer, 1966).

*Erlei, Mathias, Leschke, Martin and Sauerland, Dirk*, Neue Institutionenökonomik, 2nd ed. (Stuttgart: Schäffer-Poeschel, 2007).

*Eriksson, Andrea*, Einheitlicher Europäischer Bankenaufsichtsmechanismus – Von den Vorschlägen der Kommission zur politischen Einigung im Rat, Wissenschaftliche Dienste Deutscher Bundestag (Berlin: Der Deutsche Bundestag, 2013).

*Europäische Zentralbank*, Die Geldpolitik der EZB, (Frankfurt am Main: EZB, 2004).

*Fassbender, Bardo*, Wissen als Grundlage staatlichen Handelns, in Isensee, Josef and Kirchhof, Paul (Eds.), Handbuch des Staatsrechts – Volume IV: Aufgaben des Staates, 3rd ed. (Heidelberg: C. F. Müller, 2006), § 76.

*Fehling, Michael*, Informelles Verwaltungshandeln, in Hoffmann-Riem, Wolfgang, Schmidt-Aßmann, Eberhard and Voßkuhle, Andreas (Eds.), Grundlagen des Verwaltungsrechts – Volume 2: Informationsordnung, Verwaltungsverfahren, Handlungsformen, 2nd ed. (München: C. H. Beck, 2012), § 38.

*Fehling, Michael*, Instrumente und Verfahren, in Fehling, Michael and Ruffert, Matthias (Eds.), Regulierungsrecht, (Tübingen: Mohr Siebeck, 2010), § 20.

*Ferber, Markus*, Die Neuordnung der Europäischen Aufsichtsstruktur., Ifo-Schnelldienst 64 (2011), pp. 9–13.

*Forsthoff, Ernst*, Lehrbuch des Allgemeinen Verwaltungsrechts – Erster Band: Allgemeiner Teil, 10th ed. (München: C. H. Beck, 1973).

*Fritsch, Michael*, Markversagen und Wirtschaftspolitik, 9th ed. (Vahlen: München 2014).

*Gärditz, Klaus Ferdinand*, Europäisches Regulierungsverwaltungsrecht auf Abwegen, Archiv des öffentliches Rechts, Vol. 135 (2010), pp. 251–288.

*Garner, Bryan A.*, (Ed.), Black's Law Dictionary, 8th ed. (Eagan: Thomson West, 2004).

*Glatzl, Stefan*, Geldpolitik und Bankenaufsicht im Konflikt, (Baden-Baden: Nomos, 2009).

*Gleeson, Simon*, International Regulation of Banking, 1st ed. (Oxford: Oxford University Press, 2010).

*Giovanoli, Mario*, Reflections on International Financial Standards as, Soft Law', 37 Essays in International Financial and Economic Law (2002), pp. 1–38.

*Grabitz, Eberhard, Hilf, Meinhard and Nettesheim, Martin* (Eds.), Das Recht der Europäischen Union: EUV/AEUV, 53rd ed. (München: C.H. Beck, 2014).

*Grande, Mauro,* Banking Regulation and supervision – developments and prospects at the global and EU levels, in Grieser, Simon G. and Heemann, Manfred (Eds.), Bankenaufsichtsrecht, (Frankfurt am Main: Frankfurt School Verlag, 2010), pp. 19–37.

*Groß, Thomas*, Die Verwaltungsorganisation als Teil organisierter Staatlichkeit, in Hoffmann-Riem, Wolfgang, Schmidt-Aßmann, Eberhard and Voßkuhle, Andreas (Eds.), Grundlagen des Verwaltungsrechts – Volume 1: Methoden, Maßstäbe, Aufgaben, Organisation, 2nd ed. (München: C. H. Beck, 2012), § 13.

*Groß, Thomas*, Das Kollegialprinzip in der Verwaltungsorganisation, (Tübingen: Mohr Siebeck, 1999).

*Groß, Thomas*, Grundzüge der organisationswissenschaftlichen Diskussion, in Schmidt-Aßmann, Eberhard and Hoffmann-Riem, Wolfgang (Eds.), Verwaltungsorganisationsrecht als Steuerungsressource, (Nomos: Baden-Baden, 1997), pp. 139–150.

*Gurlit, Elke*, The ECB's relationship to EBA, Europäische Zeitschrift für Wirtschaftsrecht (2014), Beilage, pp. 14–18.

*Haas, Tillmann*, Die Bundesanstalt für Finanzdienstleistungsaufsicht, in Grieser, Simon G. and Heemann, Manfred (Eds.), Bankenaufsichtsrecht, (Frankfurt am Main: Frankfurt School Verlag, 2010), pp. 59–68.

*Haratsch, Andreas, Koenig, Christian and Pechstein, Matthias* (Eds.), Europarecht, 9th ed. (Tübingen: Mohr Siebeck, 2014).

*Häde, Ulrich*, Jenseits der Effizienz: Wer kontrolliert die Kontrolleure? – Demokratische Verantwortlichkeit und rechtsstaatliche Kontrolle der europäischen Finanzaufsichtsbehörden, Europäische Zeitschrift für Wirtschaftsrecht (2011), pp. 662–666.

*Hecker, Jan*, Marktoptimierende Wirtschaftsaufsicht, Öffentlich-rechtliche Probleme staatlicher Wirtschaftsintervention zur Steigerung der Funktionsfähigkeit des Marktes, (Tübingen, Mohr Siebeck, 2007).

*Hellwig, Martin*, Finanzmarktregulierung – Welche Regelungen empfehlen sich für den deutschen und europäischen Finanzsektor?, Verhandlungen des 68. Deutschen Juristentages 2010 in Berlin, (München: C. H. Beck, 2010), Gutachten E.

*Herdegen, Matthias*, Europäische Bankenunion. Wege zu einer einheitlichen Bankenaufsicht, Wertpapiermitteilungen (2012), pp. 1889–1898.

*Herdegen, Matthias*, Bankenaufsicht im Europäischen Verbund – Banking Supervision within the European Union, (Berlin: De Gruyter, 2010).

*Herzmann, Karsten*, Konsultationen, (Tübingen: Mohr Siebeck, 2010).

*Hirshleifer, Jack and Riley, John,* The analytics of uncertainty and information, (Cambridge: Cambridge University Press, 1992).

*Höfling, Wolfram*, Finanzmarktregulierung – Welche Regelungen empfehlen sich für den deutschen und europäischen Finanzsektor?, Verhandlungen des 68. Deutschen Juristentages 2010 in Berlin, (München: C. H. Beck, 2010), Gutachten F.

*Höpfner, Birgit*, CRD IV – Neues Regulierungspaket für Banken in Kraft, BaFin Journal 1/2014, pp. 21–25.

*Hoffmann-Riem, Wolfgang*, Eigenständigkeit der Verwaltung, in Hoffmann-Riem, Wolfgang, Schmidt-Aßmann, Eberhard and Voßkuhle, Andreas (Eds.), Grundlagen des Verwaltungsrechts – Band 1: Methoden, Maßstäbe, Aufgaben, Organisation, 2nd ed. (München: C. H. Beck, 2012), § 10.

*Hoffmann-Riem, Wolfgang*, Einleitende Problemskizze, in Hoffmann-Riem, Wolfgang and Schmidt-Aßmann, Eberhard (Eds.), Verwaltungsrecht in der Informationsgesellschaft, (Baden-Baden: Nomos, 2000), pp. 9–58.

*Holznagel, Bernd*, Informationsbeziehungen in und zwischen Behörden, in Hoffmann-Riem, Wolfgang, Schmidt-Aßmann, Eberhard and Voßkuhle, Andreas (Eds.), Grundlagen des Verwaltungsrechts – Volume 2: Informationsordnung, Verwaltungsverfahren, Handlungsformen, 2nd ed. (München: C. H. Beck, 2012), § 24.

*Honold, Eduard*, Die Bankenaufsicht, (Stuttgart: Selbstdruck, 1956).

*Huber, Peter M.*, Öffentliches Wirtschaftsrecht, in Schoch, Friedrich (Ed.), Besonderes Verwaltungsrecht, 15th ed. (Berlin: De Gruyter, 2013), pp. 309–432.

*Humm, Hubert*, Bankenaufsicht und Währungssicherung, (Berlin: Duncker & Humblot, 1989).

*Jansen, Dorothea and Schubert, Klaus*, Netzwerkanalyse, Netzwerkforschung und Politikproduktion: Ansätze zur ‚cross-fertilization', in Jansen, Dorothea and Schubert, Klaus (Eds.), Netzwerke und Politikproduktion. Konzepte, Methoden, Perspektiven, (Marburg: Schüren, 1995), pp. 9–23.

Jestaedt, Matthias, Demokratieprinzip und Kondominialverwaltung – Entscheidungsteilhabe Privater an der öffentlichen Verwaltung auf dem Prüfstand des Verfassungsprinzips Demokratie, (Berlin: Duncker & Humblot, 1993).

Jörgens, Stefan, Die koordinierte Aufsicht über europaweit tätige Banken (Baden-Baden: Nomos, 2000).

*Junker, Johannes*, Gewährleistungsaufsicht über Wertpapierdienstleistungsunternehmen – Die hoheitliche Regulierung gesellschaftlicher Selbstregulierung durch die Bundesanstalt für Finanzdienstleistungsaufsicht, (Berlin: Duncker & Humblot, 2003).

*Kämmerer, Jörn Axel*, Bahn frei der Bankenunion? – Die neuen Aufsichtsbefugnisse der EZB im Lichte der EU-Kompetenzordnung, Neue Zeitschrift für Verwaltungsrecht (2013), pp. 830–836.

*Kämmerer, Jörn Axel*, Das neue Europäische Finanzaufsichtssystem (ESFS) – Modell für eine europäisierte Verwaltungsarchitektur, Neue Zeitschrift für Verwaltungsrecht (2011), pp. 1281–1288.

*Kahl, Wolfgang*, Die Staatsaufsicht – Entstehung, Wandel und Neubestimmung unter besonderer Berücksichtigung der Aufsicht über Gemeinden, (Tübingen: Mohr Siebeck, 2000).

*Kindler, Peter*, Finanzkrise und Finanzmarktregulierung – Ein Zwischenruf zum 68. Deutschen Juristentag, Neue Juristische Wochenschrift (2010), pp. 2465–2469.

*Kirchhof, Paul*, Mittel staatlichen Handelns, in Iseensee, Josef and Kirchhof, Paul (Eds.), Handbuch des Staatsrechts – Volume V: Rechtsquellen, Organisation, Finanzen, 3rd ed. (Heidelberg: C. F. Müller, 2007), § 99.

*Kluth, Winfried*, Gegenstand und Begriff des Verwaltungsorganisationsrechts, in Wolff, Hans Julius, Bachof, Otto, Stober, Rolf and Kluth, Winfried (Eds.), Verwaltungsrecht II, 7th ed. (München: C. H. Beck, 2010), § 79.

*Knieps, Günter,* Wettbewerbsökonomie. Regulierungstheorie, Industrieökonomie, Wettbewerbspolitik, 3rd ed. (Berlin/Heidelberg: Springer, 2008).

*Knight, Frank H.*, Risk, Uncertainty and Profit, (New York: Harper and Row, 1971).
*König, Elke*, Einheitlicher Aufsichtsmechanismus, BaFin Journal 5/2014, pp. 18–21.
*Kosiol, Erich*, Organisation der Unternehmung, 2nd ed. (Wiesbaden: Gabler, 1976).
*Kovacic, William E.*, Distinguished essay: Good agency practice and the implementation of competition law, in Hermann, Christoph, Krajewski, Markus and Terhechte, Jörg Philipp (Eds.), European Yearbook of International Economic Law Volume 4 (Heidelberg: Springer, 2013), pp. 3–22.
*Krebs, Walter*, Verwaltungsorganisation, in Iseensee, Josef and Kirchhof, Paul (Eds.), Handbuch des Staatsrechts – Volume V: Rechtsquellen, Organisation, Finanzen, 3rd ed. (Heidelberg: C.F. Müller, 2007), § 108.
*Krebs, Walter*, Die juristische Methode im Verwaltungsrecht, in Schmidt-Aßmann, Eberhard and Hoffmann-Riem, Wolfgang (Eds.), Methoden der Verwaltungswissenschaft, (Nomos: Baden-Baden, 2004), pp. 209–221.
*Larenz, Karl*, Methodenlehre der Rechtswissenschaft, 6th ed. (Berlin: Springer, 1991).
*Lepsius, Oliver*, Steuerungsdiskussion, Systemtheorie und Parlamentarismuskritik, (Tübingen: Mohr Siebeck, 1999).
*Leschke, Martin*, Regulierungstheorie aus ökonomischer Sicht, in Fehling, Michael and Ruffert, Matthias (Eds.), Regulierungsrecht, (Tübingen: Mohr Siebeck, 2010), § 5.
*Loeser, Roman*, System des Verwaltungsrechts, Volume 2, (Baden-Baden: Nomos, 1994).
*Ludwigs, Markus*, Die Bundesnetzagentur auf dem Weg zur independant agency? – Europarechtliche Anstöße und verfassungsrechtliche Grenzen, Die Verwaltung (2011), pp. 41–74.
*Luhmann, Niklas*, Funktionen und Folgen formaler Organisationen, 2nd ed. (Berlin, Duncker & Humblot, 1972).
*Majone, Giandomenico*, The regulatory state and its legitimacy problems, 22 West European Politics, (1999), pp. 1–24.
*Majone, Giandomenico*, The new European Agencies: regulation by information, 4 Journal of European Public Policy, (1997), pp. 262–275.
*Majone, Giandomenico*, Regulation and its modes, in Majone, Giandomenico (Ed.), Regulating Europe, (London/New York: Routledge, 1996), pp. 9–27.
*Manger-Nestler, Cornelia and Böttner, Robert*, Ménage à trois? – Zur gewandelten Rolle der EZB im Spannungsfeld zwischen Geldpolitik, Finanzaufsicht und Fiskalpolitik, Europarecht 2014, pp. 621–638.
*Manger-Nestler, Cornelia*, Interaction for Monetary and Financial Stability: Central Banks as Main Actors in the Global Financial System, in Hermann, Christoph, Krajewski, Markus and Terhechte, Jörg Philipp (Eds.), European Yearbook of International Economic Law Volume 5 (Heidelberg: Springer, 2014), pp. 33–65.
*Mankiw, N. Gregory and Taylor, Mark P.* (Eds.), Economics, 2nd ed. (Andover: South-Western Cengage Learning, 2011).
*Masing, Johannes*, Soll das Recht der Regulierungsverwaltung übergreifend geregelt werden?, Gutachten für den 66.Deutschen Juristentag (2006), Gutachten D.
*Masing, Johannes*, Transparente Verwaltung: Konturen eines Informationsverwaltungsrechts, 63 Veröffentlichungen der Vereinigung der deutschen Staatsrechtslehrer (2003), pp. 377–441.
*Masing, Johannes*, Grundstrukturen eines Regulierungsverwaltungsrechts, Die Verwaltung (2003), pp. 1–32.
*Mayntz, Renate*, Governance im modernen Staat, in Benz, Arthur (Ed.), Governance – Regieren in komplexen Regelsystemen, (Wiesbaden: VS Verlag für Sozialwissenschaften, 2004), pp. 65–76.
*Mayntz, Renate*, New challenges to governance theory, in Bang, Henrik P. (Ed.), Governance as social and political communication, (Manchester: Manchester University Press, 2003), pp. 27–40.
*Mayntz, Renate*, Soziologie der öffentlichen Verwaltung, (Heidelberg: C.F. Müller, 1978).
*Mayntz, Renate*, Soziologie der Organisation, (Reinbeck bei Hamburg: Rowohlt, 1963).

*Möllers, Christoph*, Materielles Recht – Verfahrensrecht – Organisationsrecht, in Trute, Hans-Heinrich, Groß, Thomas, Röhl, Hans Christian and Möllers, Christoph (Eds.), Allgemeines Verwaltungsrecht zur Tragfähigkeit eines Konzepts, (Tübingen: Mohr Siebeck, 2008), pp. 489–512.

*Möllers, Christoph*, Der vermisste Leviathan – Staatstheorie in der Bundesrepublik, (Frankfurt am Main: Suhrkamp, 2008).

*Möllers, Christoph*, Gewaltengliederung, (Tübingen: Mohr Siebeck, 2006).

*Möllers, Christoph*, Transnationale Behördenkooperation – Verfassungs- und völkerrechtliche Probleme transnationaler administrativer Standardsetzung, 65 Zeitschrift für ausländisches öffentliches Recht und Völkerrecht (2005), pp. 351–389.

*Möllers, Christoph*, Netzwerk als Kategorie des Organisationsrechts. Zur juristischen Beschreibung dezentraler Steuerung, in Oebbecke, Janbernd (Ed.), Nicht-normative Steuerung in dezentralen Systemen, (Opladen: Franz Steiner Verlag, 2005), pp. 285–302.

*Neumann, Kerstin*, The supervisory powers of national authorities and cooperation with the ECB – a new epoch of banking supervision, Europäische Zeitschrift für Wirtschaftsrecht (2014), Beilage, pp. 9–14.

*Nicolaysen, Gert*, Rechtsfragen der Währungsunion, (Berlin/New York: Springer), 1993.

*North, Douglas C.*, Institutions, institutional change and economic performance, (Cambridge: Cambridge University Press, 1991).

*Ohler, Christoph,* Bankenaufsichtsrecht, in Ehlers, Dirk, Fehling, Michael and Pünder, Hermann (Eds.), Besonderes Verwaltungsrecht – Volume 1: Öffentliches Wirtschaftsrecht, 3rd ed. (Heidelberg: C.F. Müller 2012), § 32.

*Ohler, Christoph,* Internationale Regulierung im Bereich der Finanzmarktaufsicht, in Möllers, Christoph, Voßkuhle, Andreas and Walter, Christian (Eds.), Internationales Verwaltungsrecht, (Tübingen: Mohr Siebeck, 2007), pp. 259–278.

*Oppermann, Thomas, Classen, Claus Dieter and Nettesheim, Martin* (Eds.), Europarecht, 6th ed. (München: C.H. Beck, 2014).

*Peuker, Enrico*, Die Anwendung nationaler Rechtsvorschriften durch Unionsorgane – ein Konstruktionsfehler der europäischen Bankenaufsicht, Juristische Zeitung (2014), pp. 764–771.

*Pitschas, Rainer and Gille, Stefanie*, Allfinanzaufsicht in der EU und in Deutschland, in Pitschas, Rainer (Ed.), Integrierte Finanzdienstleistungsaufsicht, Bankensystem und Bankenaufsicht vor den Herausforderungen der Europäischen Wirtschafts- und Währungsunion, (Berlin: Duncker & Humblot, 2002), pp. 219–255.

*Pitschas, Rainer*, Allgemeines Verwaltungsrecht als Teil der öffentlichen Informationsordnung, in Hoffmann-Riem, Wolfgang, Schmidt-Aßmann, Eberhard and Schuppert, Gunnar-Folke (Eds.) Reform des Allgemeinen Verwaltungsrechts – Grundfragen, (Baden-Baden: Nomos, 1993), pp. 219–305.

*Philips, Louis*, The economics of imperfect information, (Cambridge: Cambridge University Press, 1988).

*Proelss, Alexander*, Das Regulierungsermessen – eine Ausprägung des behördlichen Letztentscheidungsrechts?, 136 Archiv des öffentlichen Rechts, (2011), pp. 402–427.

*Prosser, Tony*, Law and the Regulators, (Oxford: Oxford University Press, 1997).

*Posner, Richard A.*, Economic Analysis of Law, 8th ed. (Austin/Boston/Chicago/New York: Wolters Kluwer International, 2011).

*Püttner, Günter*, Verwaltungslehre, 4th ed. (München: C. H. Beck, 2007).

*Rengeling, Hans-Werner*, Rechtsgrundsätze beim Verwaltungsvollzug des Europäischen Gemeinschaftsrechts. Zu den Grundlagen des Verwaltungsvollzuges sowie zur Theorie und Konkretisierung der Rechtsgrundsätze unter besonderer Berücksichtigung der Rechtsvergleichung, Kölner Schriften zum Europarecht 27 (Köln: Carl Heymanns Verlag, 1977).

*Richter, Rudolf and Furobotn, Eirik*, Neue Institutionenökonomik – Eine Einführung und kritische Würdigung, 4th ed. (Tübingen: Mohr Siebeck, 2010).

*Ritter, Ernst-Hasso*, Das Recht als Steuerungsmedium im kooperativen Staat, in Grimm, Dieter (Ed.), Wachsende Staatsaufgaben – Sinkende Steuerungsfähigkeit des Rechts, (Baden-Baden: Nomos, 1990).

*Röhl, Hans Christian*, Ausgewählte Verwaltungsverfahren, in Hoffmann-Riem, Wolfgang, Schmidt-Aßmann, Eberhard and Voßkuhle, Andreas (Eds.), Grundlagen des Verwaltungsrechts – Volume 2: Informationsordnung, Verwaltungsverfahren, Handlungsformen, 2nd ed. (München: C. H. Beck, 2012), § 30.

*Röhl, Hans Christian*, Finanzmarkaufsicht, in Fehling, Michael and Ruffert, Matthias (Eds.), Regulierungsrecht, (Tübingen: Mohr Siebeck, 2010), § 18.

*Röhl, Hans Christian*, Der rechtliche Kontext der Wissenserzeugung, in Röhl (Ed.), Wissen zur kognitiven Dimension des Rechts, Die Verwaltung Beiheft 9 (2010), pp. 65–88.

*Ruffert, Matthias*, Grundfragen der Wirtschaftsregulierung, in Ehlers, Dirk, Fehling, Michael and Pünder, Hermann (Eds.), Besonderes Verwaltungsrecht – Volume 1: Öffentliches Wirtschaftsrecht, 3rd ed. (Heidelberg: C.F. Müller 2012), § 21.

*Ruffert, Matthias*, Begriff, in Fehling, Michael and Ruffert, Matthias (Eds.), Regulierungsrecht, (Tübingen: Mohr Siebeck, 2010), § 7.

*Ruffert, Matthias*, Verselbständigte Verwaltungseinheiten: Ein europäischer Megatrend im Vergleich, in Trute, Hans-Heinrich, Groß, Thomas, Röhl, Hans Christian and Möllers, Christoph (Eds.), Allgemeines Verwaltungsrecht – zur Tragfähigkeit eines Konzepts, (Tübingen: Mohr Siebeck, 2008), pp. 431–457.

*Ruffert, Matthias*, Perspektiven des Internationalen Verwaltungsrechts, in Möllers, Christoph, Voßkuhle, Andreas and Walter, Christian (Eds.), Internationales Verwaltungsrecht – Eine Analyse anhand von Referenzgebieten, (Tübingen: Mohr Siebeck, 2007), pp. 395–419.

*Ruffert, Matthias*, Regulierung im System des Verwaltungsrechts – Grundstrukturen des Privatisierungsfolgerechts der Telekommunikation und Post, 124 Archiv des öffentlichen Rechts (1999), pp. 237–281.

*Ruthig, Josef and Storr, Stefan* (Eds.), Öffentliches Wirtschaftsrecht, (Heidelberg: C. F. Müller, 2012).

*Sacarcelik, Osman*, Europäische Bankenunion: Rechtliche Rahmenbedingungen und Herausforderungen der einheitlichen europäischen Bankenaufsicht, Zeitschrift für Bank- und Kapitalmarktrecht (2013), pp. 353–360.

*Sachverständigenrat zur Begutachtung der gesamtwirtschaftlichen Entwicklung*, Gegen eine rückwärtsgewandte Wirtschaftspolitik – Jahresgutachten 2013 / 14 (Paderborn: Bonifatius GmbH Buch-Druck Verlag, 2013).

*Schäfer, Thomas and Rolker, Andreas*, Bankenaufsicht im Spannungsfeld von Regulierung und Wettbewerb, in Grieser, Simon G. and Heemann, Manfred (Eds.), Bankenaufsicht nach der Finanzmarktkrise, (Frankfurt am Main: Frankfurt School Verlag, 2011), pp. 3–23.

*Scharpf, Fritz W.*, Does Organization Matter? Task Structure and Interaction in the Ministerial Bureaucracy, Organization and Administrative Sciences (1977), pp. 149–168.

*Scherzberg, Arno*, Wissen, Nichtwissen und Ungewißheit im Recht, in Engel, Christoph, Halfmann, Jost and Schulte, Martin (Eds.), Wissen – Nichtwissen – Unsicheres Wissen, (Baden-Baden: Nomos, 2002), pp. 114–144.

*Scherzberg, Arno*, Die öffentliche Verwaltung als informationelle Organisation, in Hoffmann-Riem, Wolfgang and Schmidt-Aßmann, Eberhard (Eds.), Verwaltungsrecht in der Informationsgesellschaft, (Baden-Baden: Nomos, 2000), pp. 195–223.

*Schmidt-Aßmann, Eberhard*, Verfassungsprinzipien für den Europäischen Verwaltungsverbund, in Hoffmann-Riem, Wolfgang, Schmidt-Aßmann, Eberhard and Voßkuhle, Andreas (Eds.), Grundlagen des Verwaltungsrechts – Volume 1: Methoden, Maßstäbe, Aufgaben, Organisation, 2nd ed. (München: C. H. Beck, 2012), § 5.

*Schmidt-Aßmann, Eberhard*, Die Ambivalenz des Wissens und die Ordnungsaufgaben des Rechts, in: Röhl, Hans Christian (Ed.), Wissen – Zur kognitiven Dimension des Rechts, Die Verwaltung Beiheft 9 (2010), pp. 39–62.

*Schmidt-Aßmann, Eberhard*, Die Herausforderungen der Verwaltungswissenschaft durch die Internationalisierung der Verwaltungsbeziehungen, 45 Der Staat (2006), pp. 315–338.
*Schmidt-Aßmann, Eberhard*, Einleitung: Der Europäische Verwaltungsverbund und die Rolle des europäischen Verwaltungsrechts, in Schmidt-Aßmann, Eberhard and Schöndorf-Haubold, Bettina (Eds.), Der Europäische Verwaltungsverbund, (Tübingen: Mohr Siebeck, 2005), pp. 1–23.
*Schmidt-Aßmann, Eberhard*, Das allgemeine Verwaltungsrecht als Ordnungsidee, 2nd ed. (Berlin/Heidelberg, Springer, 2004).
*Schmidt-Aßmann, Eberhard*, Der Europäische Verwaltungsverbund zwischen Kooperation und Hierarchie, in Cremer, Hans-Joachim, Giegerich, Thomas, Richter, Dagmar and Zimmermann, Andreas (Eds.), Tradition und Weltoffenheit des Rechts – Festschrift für Helmut Steinberger, (Berlin/Heidelberg/New York, Springer, 2002), pp. 1375–1399.
*Schmidt-Aßmann, Eberhard*, Perspektiven einer Systembildung, in Hoffmann-Riem, Wolfgang and Schmidt-Aßmann, Eberhard (Eds.), Verwaltungsrecht in der Informationsgesellschaft, (Baden-Baden: Nomos, 2000), pp. 405–432.
*Schmidt-Aßmann, Eberhard*, Verwaltungsorganisationsrecht als Steuerungsressource – Eine Einführung, in Schmidt-Aßmann, Eberhard and Hoffmann-Riem, Wolfgang (Eds.), Verwaltungsorganisationsrecht als Steuerungsressource, (Baden-Baden: Nomos, 1997), pp. 9–63.
*Schmidt-Aßmann, Eberhard*, Verwaltungskooperation und Verwaltungskooperationsrecht in der Europäischen Gemeinschaft, Europarecht (1996), pp. 270–301.
*Schmidt-Preuß, Matthias*, Das Regulierungsrecht als interdisziplinäre Disziplin – am Beispiel des Energierechts, in Baur, Jürgen F., Sandrock, Otto, Scholtka, Boris and Shapiro, Amos (Eds.), Festschrift für Gunther Kühne zum 70.Geburtstag, (Frankfurt am Main: Verlag Recht und Wissenschaft, 2010), pp. 329–342.
*Schneider, Uwe H.*, Inconsistencies and unsolved Problems in the European Banking Union, Europäische Zeitschrift für Wirtschaftsrecht (2013), pp. 452–457.
*Schoch, Friedrich*, Öffentlich-rechtliche Rahmenbedingungen einer Informationsordnung, 57 Veröffentlichungen der Vereinigung der Deutschen Staatsrechtslehrer (1998), pp. 158–215.
*Schuppert, Gunnar Folke*, Verwaltungsorganisation und Verwaltungsorganisationsrecht als Steuerungsressource, in Hoffmann-Riem, Wolfgang, Schmidt-Aßmann, Eberhard and Voßkuhle, Andreas (Eds.), Grundlagen des Verwaltungsrechts – Volume 1: Methoden, Maßstäbe, Aufgaben, Organisation, 2nd ed. (München: C. H. Beck, 2012), § 16.
*Schuppert, Gunnar Folke*, Verwaltungswissenschaft – Verwaltung, Verwaltungsrecht, Verwaltungslehre, (Baden-Baden: Nomos, 2000).
*Schuppert, Gunnar Folke*, Verwaltungsrechtswissenschaft als Steuerungswissenschaft. Zur Steuerung des Verwaltungshandelns durch Verwaltungsrecht, in Schmidt-Aßmann, Eberhard, Hoffmann-Riem, Wolfgang and Schuppert, Gunnar Folke (Eds.), Zur Reform des Allgemeinen Verwaltungsrechts, (Baden-Baden: Nomos, 1993), pp. 67–114.
*Shapiro, Amos*, The problems of independent agencies in the United States and the European Union, 4 Journal of European Public Policy (1997), pp. 276–291.
*Schuster, Gunnar*, The banking supervisory competences and powers of the ECB, Europäische Zeitschrift für Wirtschaftsrecht (2014), Beilage, pp. 3–9.
*Siegel, Thorsten*, Entscheidungsfindung im Verwaltungsverbund – Horizontale Entscheidungsvernetzung und vertikale Entscheidungsstufung im nationalen und europäischen Verwaltungsverbund, (Tübingen: Mohr Siebeck, 2009).
*Spiecker gen. Döhmann, Indra*, Das Verwaltungsrecht zwischen klassischem dogmatischen Verständnis und steuerungswissenschaftlichem Anspruch, Deutsches Verwaltungsblatt (2007), pp. 1074–1084.
*Spiecker gen. Döhmann, Indra*, Die staatliche Informationsgewinnung im Mehrebenensystem – ein Überblick, in Oebbecke, Janbernd (Ed.), Nicht-normative Steuerung in dezentralen Systemen, (Opladen: Franz Steiner Verlag, 2005), pp. 253–285.
*Stevenson, Angus*, Oxford dictionary of English, 3rd ed. (Oxford: Oxford University Press, 2010).

*Stober Rolf*, Der Begriff der öffentlichen Verwaltung, in Wolff, Hans Julius, Bachof, Otto, Stober, Rolf and Kluth, Winfried (Eds.), Verwaltungsrecht I, 12th ed. (München: C. H. Beck, 2007), § 3.

*Stober Rolf*, Wirtschaftsaufsicht und Bankenaufsicht, in Pitschas, Rainer (Ed.) Integrierte Finanzdienstleistungsaufsicht, Bankensystem und Bankenaufsicht vor den Herausforderungen der Europäischen Wirtschafts- und Währungsunion, (Berlin: Duncker & Humblot, 2002), pp. 21–64.

*Streinz, Rudolf*, Europarecht, 9th ed. (Heidelberg: C.F. Müller, 2012).

*Terhechte, Jörg Philipp*, Einführung: Das Verwaltungsrecht der Europäischen Union als Gegenstand rechtswissenschaftlicher Forschung – Entwicklungslinien, Prinzipien und Perspektiven in Terhechte, Jörg Philipp (Ed.), Verwaltungsrecht der Europäischen Union, (Baden-Baden: Nomos, 2010), § 1.

*Thiele, Alexander*, Finanzaufsicht, (Tübingen: Mohr Siebeck, 2014).

*Thieme, Werner*, Verwaltungslehre, 4th ed. (Köln/Berlin: Carl Heymanns Verlag, 1984).

*Trute, Hans-Heinrich*, Die demokratische Legitimation der Verwaltung, in Hoffmann-Riem, Wolfgang, Schmidt-Aßmann, Eberhard and Voßkuhle, Andreas (Eds.), Grundlagen des Verwaltungsrechts – Volume 1: Methoden, Maßstäbe, Aufgaben, Organisation, 2nd ed. (München: C. H. Beck, 2012), § 6.

*Trute, Hans-Heinrich*, Wissen – Einleitende Bemerkungen, in Röhl, Hans Christian (Ed.), Wissen zur kognitiven Dimension des Rechts, Die Verwaltung Beiheft 9 (2010), pp. 11–38.

*Trute, Hans-Heinrich*, Methodik der Herstellung und Darstellung verwaltungsrechtlicher Entscheidungen in Schmidt-Aßmann, Eberhard and Hoffmann-Riem, Wolfgang (Eds.), Methoden der Verwaltungsrechtswissenschaft, (Baden-Baden: Nomos, 2004), pp. 293–325.

*Trute, Hans-Heinrich*, Verantwortungsteilung als Schlüsselbegriff eines sich verändernden Verhältnisses von öffentlichem und privatem Sektor, in Schuppert, Gunnar Folke (Eds.), Jenseits von Privatisierung und „schlankem“ Staat, (Baden-Baden: Nomos, 1999), pp. 13–45.

*Trute, Hans-Heinrich*, Die Funktionen von Organisationen und ihre Abbildung im Recht, in Schmidt-Aßmann, Eberhard and Hoffmann-Riem, Wolfgang (Eds.), Verwaltungsorganisationsrecht als Steuerungsressource, (Baden-Baden: Nomos, 1997), pp. 249–295.

*Trute, Hans-Heinrich*, Die Verwaltung und das Verwaltungsrecht zwischen gesellschaftlicher Selbstregulierung und staatlicher Steuerung, Deutsches Verwaltungsblatt (1996), pp. 950–964.

*von Hayek, Friedrich August*, Der Wettbewerb als Entdeckungsverfahren, (Kiel: Institut für Weltwirtschaft, 1968).

*Vesting, Thomas*, Die Bedeutung von Information und Kommunikation für die verwaltungsrechtliche Systembildung, in Hoffmann-Riem, Wolfgang, Schmidt-Aßmann, Eberhard and Voßkuhle, Andreas (Eds.), Grundlagen des Verwaltungsrechts – Volume 2: Informationsordnung, Verwaltungsverfahren, Handlungsformen, 2nd ed. (München: C. H. Beck, 2012), § 20.

*Vesting, Thomas*, Zwischen Gewährleistungsstaat und Minimalstaat, in Hoffmann-Riem, Wolfgang and Schmidt-Aßmann, Eberhard (Eds.), Verwaltungsrecht in der Informationsgesellschaft, (Baden-Baden: Nomos, 2000), pp. 101–131.

*Voßkuhle, Andreas*, Expertise und Verwaltung, in Trute, Hans-Heinrich, Groß, Thomas, Röhl, Hans Christian and Möllers, Christoph (Eds.), Allgemeines Verwaltungsrecht zur Tragfähigkeit eines Konzepts, (Tübingen: Mohr Siebeck, 2008), pp. 637–664.

*Voßkuhle, Andreas*, Sachverständige Beratung des Staates, in Isensee, Josef and Kirchhof, Paul (Eds.), Handbuch des Staatsrechts – Volume III: Demokratie – Bundesorgane, 3rd ed. (Heidelberg: C. F. Müller, 2005), § 43.

*Waigel, Christian*, Deutsche Bankenaufsicht und internationale Bankenaufsicht, in Grieser, Simon G. and Heemann, Manfred (Eds.), Bankenaufsichtsrecht, (Frankfurt am Main: Frankfurt School Verlag, 2010), pp. 39–58.

*Waschbusch, Gerd and Rolle, Andrea*, Testament von Banken. Sanierungs- und Abwicklungspläne im Rahmen aktueller Reformprozesse, Wirtschafswissenschaftliches Studium, 42 (2013), pp. 453–455.

*Weaver, Kent R. and Rockman, Bert A.*, Assessing the effects of institutions: When and how do institutions matter, in Weaver, Kent R. and Rockman, Bert A. (Eds.), Do institutions matter? Government capabilities in the United States and abroad, (Washington D.C.: Brookings Institute, 1993), pp. 1–41.

*Wellerdt, Alexander*, Organisation der Regulierungsverwaltung, forthcoming.

*Weiß, Wolfgang*, Der Europäische Verwaltungsverbund, (Berlin: Duncker & Humblot, 2010).

*Williamson, Oliver*, The economic institutions of capitalism – Firms; Markets, Relational Contracting, (New York/London, Free Press, 1985).

*Williamson, Oliver*, Transaction-cost economics, 3 Journal of Law and Economics (1979), pp. 233–261.

*Willke, Helmut*, Supervision des Staates, (Frankfurt am Main: Suhrkamp, 1997).

*Wöhe, Günter and Döring, Ulrich* (Eds.), Einführung in die Allgemeine Betriebswirtschaftslehre, 25th ed. (München: Vahlen, 2013).

*Wojcik, Karl-Philipp and Ceyssens, Jan*, Der einheitliche EU-Bankenabwicklungsmechanismus: Vollendung der Bankenunion, Schutz des Steuerzahlers, Europäische Zeitschrift für Wirtschaftsrecht (2014), pp. 893–898.

*Wolfers, Benedikt and Voland, Thomas*, Europäische Zentralbank und Bankenaufsicht – Rechtsgrundlage und demokratische Kontrolle des Single Supervisory Mechanism, Zeitschrift für Bank- und Kapitalmarktrecht (2014), pp. 177–185.

*Wollenschläger, Burkard*, Wissensgenerierung im Verfahren, (Tübingen: Mohr Siebeck, 2009).

*Wymeersch, Eddy*, The new European financial regulatory bodies, 76 Revue bancaire et financière (2012), pp. 28–39.

*Zeitler, Franz-Christoph*, Finanzmarktkrise und Bankenaufsicht, in Grieser, Simon G. and Heemann, Manfred (Eds.), Bankenaufsichtsrecht – Entwicklungen und Perspektiven, (Frankfurt am Main: Frankfurt School Verlag, 2010), pp. 3–15.

*Ziekow, Jan*, Öffentliches Wirtschaftsrecht, 3rd ed. (München: C. H. Beck, 2013).

*Zimmer; Daniel*, Finanzmarktregulierung – Welche Regelungen empfehlen sich für den deutschen und europäischen Finanzsektor?, Verhandlungen des 68. Deutschen Juristentages 2010 in Berlin, (München: C. H. Beck, 2010), Gutachten G.

MIX
Papier aus verantwortungsvollen Quellen
Paper from responsible sources
FSC® C105338

If you have any concerns about our products,
you can contact us on
**ProductSafety@springernature.com**

In case Publisher is established outside the EU,
the EU authorized representative is:
**Springer Nature Customer Service Center GmbH**
**Europaplatz 3, 69115 Heidelberg, Germany**

Printed by Libri Plureos GmbH
in Hamburg, Germany